Buoyant

Early Praise for Buoyant

"An inspiring story of friendship, triumph, and loss over a background of peace and beauty. Stunningly penned as Doherty describes the Chesapeake Bay in spectacular detail. *Buoyant* left me with renewed empathy as a physician, of appreciating a person beyond their disease, and underscoring the enormous impact that each word, action, and decision has on a patient's life."

—Nandita S. Scott, MD FACC
Director of Cardiovascular Medicine
Massachusetts General Hospital

"To put it simply, *Buoyant: What Held Us Up When Our Bodies Let Us Down* is one of the most beautiful books I've ever had the pleasure of reading. A rare combination of introspection, clear-eyed honesty, nostalgia, love, elation, and sadness. Janet's story is told so wonderfully and honestly, I am absolutely certain that she would have loved it as much as I did."

—Janet's husband Steve

"I have been struck by the intense connection with nature that those with chronic or terminal illness develop, particularly with flora and fauna, deriving comfort and spiritual sustenance from newfound appreciation of the beauty of this world and its eternal patterns and rhythms. This insight is transferable to others, and that gift enriches the wholeness and depth of the human spirit. What a remarkable way to turn personal loss into growth of self and those we hold dear.

This book is full of color and sound and texture and love. Yet Doherty doesn't pull any punches. She teaches us the pain wrought by the careless remarks and prolonged stares of strangers and the dismissive pronouncements of professionals. As a reader, you will share the frustration of an illness burden that is invisible to others and the terror of living with life-threatening conditions. These are all important lessons for each of us, particularly those in health care.

Each of us is a tiny, vulnerable organism like those microscopic beings Doherty's students found in streams, part of a beautiful cosmos that we are allowed to enjoy but for a short time. Realizing that makes us grateful, compassionate, and generous."

—Patricia Czapp, MD

Buoyant
by Dotty Holcomb Doherty

Editor
Sandra Olivetti Martin
New Bay Books
Fairhaven, Maryland
NewBayBooks@gmail.com

Design by Suzanne Shelden
Shelden Studios
Prince Frederick, Maryland
sheldenstudios@comcast.net

Cover Photo:
"Sunrise Over South River Ice," by Dotty Holcomb Doherty

A Note on Type: Cover and section heads are set in ITC Bookman Std Open Type. The text font is ITC Bookman Std Light Open Type.

Library of Congress
Cataloging-in-Publication Data

ISBN 978-1-7348866-5-8

Printed in the United States of America

First Edition

Buoyant

What Held Us Up
When Our Bodies Let Us Down

Dotty Holcomb Doherty

New Bay Books

Dedication

For Jonathan,
my forever love

There is something infinitely healing
in the repeated refrains of nature–
the assurance that dawn comes after night,
and spring after the winter.

from *The Sense of Wonder* by Rachel Carson
Copyright © 1956 by Rachel L. Carson
Reprinted by permission of Frances Collin, Trustee

Table of Contents

PART 2

we meet

PART 3
we part

epilogue

Introduction

On March 16, 2008, I visited my friend Janet, a regular event since 2005. We had begun getting together when fatigue from MS tore me away from high school science teaching, and her self-consciousness about her cancer-distorted face sequestered her at home. A report on the radio that day about a man's cancer story and his new memoir had intrigued me, so I told her about it. Janet's response: "Would you write mine?"

I practically leapt into her lap.

After teaching ended, I'd found writing, though the journey was laden with self-doubt. Mentors and editors buoyed me, and my features and personal essays were carried in two local publications. Janet loved my writing, and she kept every copy of the *Bay Weekly* and *What's Up! Annapolis* that held one of my stories.

Prior to Janet's request, I'd already been composing essays about her after our weekly visits. They allowed me writing practice and acted as a journal of our time together, though they were never shown or admitted to Janet. Now permission was granted. That night I ordered a little digital tape recorder (no cell phones yet), and our visits filled with my questions and her detailed answers.

Initially, my writing took a wrong path. I chronicled her history, but it felt as though an outsider were peering in through a window. Our friendship was important, yet early readers asked why my story was not part of the manuscript. I found the right path when the characters of Janet and Dotty carried the narrative. The journey took me thirteen years.

Writing, like my other passion, wildlife photography, allows endless learning and creativity. Every sentence, word choice, scene depiction, and plotline keeps me firing on all cylinders. The editing process requires perpetual letting go and recreating until a point is reached where you say, this is my best. *Buoyant* gave me purpose and taught me story-telling. More deeply, it taught me about myself.

This book is based on Janet's true story. Dates of surgeries and major events are accurate, though liberty was taken in moving some conversations and minor events to improve flow. Names of her doctors and researchers have been changed to protect their privacy.

In developing the character of Janet, I relied on the real Janet, my time with her, plus the stories told to me by her husband Steve, daughter Stephanie, and sisters Lynn and Donna. All main characters are first names only at the request of the family. This story could not have been told without all their permissions and generosity, for which I am truly grateful. Any errors or misrepresentations are mine alone.

—Dotty Holcomb Doherty

prologue

1

Fantastical Life

Dotty

DECEMBER 2001

The prow of my kayak cuts through cold water, colder air. Rafts of migratory ducks dive and dabble for breakfast; the flute-like calls of tundra swans haunt the stillness. No other boaters in sight. The quiet is intoxicating.

Heading out over the green water of the Chesapeake Bay, I tow a foot-long plankton net behind my kayak, hoping to collect specimens for my high school biology students. For twenty minutes, the push-pull of my arms propels me in a wide slow circle, then towards shore to rest for a moment and simply drift. But when I haul in the net to check the small collecting jar, my heart sinks. The jar looks empty. I know microscopic plankton should be thriving here, but the clarity of the water sets off a niggling irrational thought. What if the water is just water?

The next day, I take the jar to my classroom wondering what critters are indeed present. Using eyedroppers, the high-schoolers and I place single drops of the Bay water on our glass slides. We set thin coverslips along one edge of our droplets and let them fall, squeezing out the air bubbles. Slides are positioned under microscope lenses and clipped in place.

What a menagerie! Gyrators, wigglers, rotators, and spinners fling themselves through our views. The green and brown and transparent zooplanktons are tentacled, ciliated, whiskered, and limbed. The biggest—a copepod looking like a one-eyed two-antennaed many-legged monster—is one millimeter long, the width of a pin. Baby barnacles, a tenth of the copepod's size, whirl by looking like hairy-legged, horned triangles. We measure them, draw pictures of them in lab books, use field guides to identify them. With the giddiness of a prospector finding gold in gravel, I pop from scope to scope marveling with my students at the fantastical life. Who knew we would find such rich diversity in single drops of clear water?

Who knows what we will encounter beneath the surface of our lives?

So much can lurk unseen.

2

Shared Life

Dotty

I lower my kayak off Janet's dock into water tinged brown after runoff from recent rains. Around us, red-winged blackbirds squeak, pipe, and whistle from the phragmites on this balmy afternoon. Though I hold the kayak steady, Janet hardly needs my help. With the confidence of a lifetime boater, she steps in and sits in the bow seat, trim in tan capris, sun hat, and life jacket over white shirt, camera hanging around her neck. No need to hand her a paddle. Her light weight makes it easy for me to manage the boat myself.

Pushing off, I aim us down the left side of Harness Creek, where the branches of sycamore, oak, sweet gum, and holly shade us with lush greens. A pair of mallards preens on a partially submerged log.

"We had a duckling once that a neighbor gave to Reid for his First Communion," Janet tells me. "He named it Chuck, but it turned out to be a girl. She loved to swim in the creek—and in Reid and Steph's kiddie pool—but one day she flew away. When a pair came back the following spring, I always believed that the female was Chuck, showing us her mate."

Gliding past the mallards, we watch the male's green head turn purple then dark blue as the light shifts. Around the bend, the creek widens. A cormorant slips beneath the surface, and moments later, emerges with a fish it deftly tosses into the air then swallows head first. Janet's whispered *wow* echoes my own. Near the mouth of the creek, two juvenile ospreys call from a platform nest. Their mom left last month. Has dad left yet or is he still catching fish for them? Will these fledglings survive this coming fall's migration, their first trip south to wintering grounds where they have never been?

Janet and I absorb the day, letting the breeze gather and swirl our hair, the sun warm our hands, the scent of late summer lift us beyond our personal realities. Janet turns to watch a black swallowtail skim by, and I see her crooked smile, her face an amalgam of scar and bulge.

My fatigue builds and I barely dip the paddle as we meander to the cove. There is no need for speed, no place to go but here. I try to be present, but my mind spirals like the brown oak leaves floating on the water's surface, vulnerable to the whims of wind and tide. How did we get to this time in our lives when our futures are so uncertain, our paths such a mystery?

PART 1

before we meet

3

Onset

Janet

MARCH 1989

Janet opens her eyes, her bedroom hazy with predawn, and realizes she's been dreaming. I actually slept, she thinks, shaking her head. She listens for Stephanie as she has each night since her birth three months ago, but the only sound is a cardinal offering his early morning song. After everything that baby has been through, finally she, we all, have some peace. If only this peace were real. Letting out a puff of breath, she pictures Reid sprawled in his big boy bed; he sleeps like he plays, full throttle in his own world.

She can just make out Steve's dark mop of hair strewn around the pillow. She nestles close, her thighs and knees tucked into the fold of his long legs, her flat stomach to his broad back. His heat seeps into her, a soothing balm.

Her mind drifts—a luxury these days—to last night's dinner when she and Steve and her older sister Lynn devoured pizza and laughed over things stupid and silly. Her tongue explores a tender part of her palate and pushes against a blister. Popping it, she feels the liquid coat her tongue, the saltiness reminding her of tears. She rolls her eyes. Once again she's burned her mouth on the hot mozzarella. Why can she never wait for it to cool? But the crust was crisp on the edges with a hint of chewiness in the middle, the pepperoni spicy just the way she likes it. She inhales and releases her breath in a deep sigh, real tears threatening as she wonders when she'll be able to eat pizza again. Eat anything again.

Her tongue probes the space between her front teeth, the gap that appeared when she was pregnant with Steph. She glances through the darkness to the top of her tall bureau where the figure of Mary stands, and whispers the words that flood in.

Hail Mary, full of grace,
the Lord is with Thee.
Blessed art Thou amongst women,
and blessed is the fruit of thy womb, Jesus.
Holy Mary, Mother of God,
pray for us sinners now and
at the hour of our death. Amen.

The words feel hollow, offering scant comfort. With a pang of guilt, she can hear her mother's voice reciting this prayer, see her hands working the rosary beads. Now all Janet can focus on is the ending...at the hour of our death...and her heart pounds.

It's today. Her heartbeats come faster, harder, the tremors thudding in her chest and expanding in circular waves like a barrage of stones volleyed onto a still lake. Squeezing her eyes shut, wishing that act alone could make it all disappear, she curls tighter into Steve and waits for the sun to rise.

Janet hears voices but doesn't want to open her eyes. The cocoon of sleep feels soft, tranquil, and she doesn't want to leave its embrace. But she can hear someone saying her name. A woman. "Janet? Janet...time to wake up." Can feel a hand touching her forearm, stroking the skin back and forth. I guess it's over, she thinks.

She opens her eyes, blinking in the bright lights. Steve and a nurse stand over her.

"Welcome back. You did great, honey," Steve says, bending to kiss her forehead. "I love you so much."

The nurse checks the monitors, the IV drip, then leaves them alone.

With her left hand, she points toward her mouth, her eyes asking her husband what her voice cannot.

"I dunno, Jan. I think it went well. Dr. Brusher should be in any moment."

She feels her fingers touching her cheek, but otherwise, no sensations, as though she's been to the dentist.

"The drugs haven't worn off, Jan. It'll be numb for a while. I think you'll be glad you can't feel anything yet."

The curtain in her ICU cubicle parts and a doctor walks in, nods to Steve, and shakes his hand. At Janet, he smiles.

"You did just fine in there. The surgery took longer than we expected, but you did really well."

Then his smile disappears.

"We performed the hemimaxillectomy to remove the tumor in your sinuses. As anticipated, we had to take out half of your palate and upper teeth. We removed all of the tumor we could. But we could not remove it all, I'm very sorry to say. The tumor was too embedded. If I had removed more, you would not have survived."

Her brain, which moments ago had felt mushy with drugs and anesthesia, pops with clarity, a Polaroid photo at its final moment of development. The tumor is still there. Half her mouth is gone, and the tumor is still there.

She watches Dr. Brusher touch Steve's elbow, guiding him toward the curtain. Though he speaks quietly, Janet can hear him. "I know these aren't the words you want to hear, but it's time to give up. There's nothing more we can do. I'm sorry, Steve, I truly am. But Janet has, maybe, six months to live."

Two days later, 2 a.m. and the next shift at Anne Arundel Medical Center in downtown Annapolis has checked in. The new ICU nurse and aide bustle in.

"How are we doing tonight, Janet?'

She wishes she could snort out loud, a facetious laugh laced with disbelief. But she holds everything inside. Numb, she wants to tell them. Numb because it's easier. Because it's easier to feel nothing than to step into her new reality.

Two words tumble through her mind. The two she cannot stop herself from repeating.

Six months. Like cottage cheese with an expiration date stamped on her forehead. Six months—twice as long as Stephanie is old. Six months—the leaves will barely have turned color. One more birthday—her 37th, one summer, maybe a couple weeks of fall. Steve says he'll figure it out, find a solution, find better doctors. But optimism seems futile, hope feels phony.

If only the doctors had listened to her twelve years ago. Oh, what energy she had back then—working, going to college, running from class to class—but that's when she felt it. A thud in the roof of her mouth, like a small ball bouncing in her sinuses onto the top of her palate with each running step. Dentists filed a tooth, did a root canal, but they never found what she was feeling. Twelve years it's been growing. Now they tell her—six months.

The nurse and the aide have things to do; they don't wait for her to answer. An earlier nurse stopped her morphine, cut her off cold, and the pain, which had been present as an undercurrent, like the shush of ocean wavelets on a summer evening, has become white-lipped breakers, each heartbeat another crash through her head so she can barely get her breath.

The nurse tells her to open her mouth.

Forceps in hand, she begins pulling out the gauze, the endless gauze packed into the cavernous space through the top of her mouth all the way to her sinuses and nose. On the left side of her mouth, her palate and upper teeth are gone.

She writhes and screams, her words garbled, but their intent clear.

"Stop...stop!" she cries out, batting at them until they pull away. "Go get Steve, get him now!"

I'm dying, she thinks as the excruciating pain envelops her, turns everything red, no longer waves but flames. I won't even live the six months. Oh, my babies. Hurry, Steve, hurry.

4

Next Steps

Janet

APRIL–JULY 1989

Now what, Janet wonders when she comes home from the hospital two weeks later. She lies on the couch looking out through the sliding glass doors, the day gray, cold, a sudden flurry of snowflakes blurring her view of the dark trees. Her tongue wants to explore the wreckage, but she wills it away. The obturator—the prosthetic palate designed to cover the gaping hole in the roof of her mouth, which allows her to swallow and speak—seems to fill her mouth, like a giant wad of worn-out gum. Far from a comfort, the foreign device plus her missing teeth serve only as a constant reminder. She is going to die.

But impending death has not squelched her sense of the absurd. That's what rises when she opens a bill for $800, sent from the dental surgeon who first located the tumor. He had asked (and they had agreed) to watch Dr. Brusher perform her hemimaxillectomy.

"Outrageous!" she yells, waving the letter at Steve, slamming it down on the kitchen counter. "I refuse to pay it. He just watched." How good it feels to seethe, to feel the fire of her bulldog nature return.

Steve calls the dental surgeon's office, ire fueling his words. Soon they receive the follow-up bill: Zero balance due.

Steve's own bulldog nature takes over as Dr. Brusher's statement, Give up, tumbles through his head. Whenever Janet looks downhearted, he repeats his promise. "I will find an answer, Jan. This is not the end. It isn't. Trust me." How she wants to believe him. She's often seen him delve into projects, but this time his focus seems to be magnified, his determination outsized, taking on extra oxygen.

Both Janet and Steve had been problem solvers at the Internal Revenue Service, expert in mathematical modeling and analysis. Janet left when Reid was born, and now Steve has put his job as an operations research analyst on hold as the IRS's first recipient of the Leave Sharing Act, his coworkers donating their leave to him. Every day for the past month, Steve has called oncologists all over the country to solve the most important problem of his life. But after two hundred and seventy doctors and a $700 phone bill, he is no closer to an answer.

So he breaks into the National Cancer Institute database.

He gets in pretending to be a doctor. But he can't decipher the truncated database. So he calls the NCI. Gabe Sudworth, in hard-tumor research, answers.

15

"Listen," Steve says. "I am a federal employee so I'll probably go to jail for this. But I don't care. I broke into your database. I need help."

Sudworth laughs. "What? I can't believe you're telling me this."

"I can't believe I'm the first to break in," Steve replies. "You have the worst security I've ever seen."

The researcher listens as Steve details Janet's situation and poses the questions he knows enough to ask after beginning an online research journey that will eventually put him ahead of the curve on therapeutics to save his wife's life. As they worry it out, Sudworth and Steve agree that the next best step—the only step—is to enter Janet in an experimental radiation trial. Neutron Radiation Treatment is available at only three labs: Lawrence Livermore National Laboratory in UCLA, Fermilab in Chicago, and University of Washington Seattle. Only Washington is conducting trials.

Steve calls Seattle. The trial is full. So he calls Sudworth again, and the researcher faxes out a letter. *I want Janet in your trial,* Sudworth writes.

The next day, Peter Gifford, the chairman of the Seattle lab, calls Steve. "Our trial is currently closed," he says. "Yet I've received a request from the National Cancer Institute to add Janet. Who do you *know*?"

"I'm desperate," Steve says.

"Let's do this. I don't usually take patients myself, but I'm intrigued by Janet's case. How soon can you get out here?"

It's Friday morning. "Monday," Steve says.

"Don't say it if you don't mean it."

"We can be there."

Steve and Janet's parents on Long Island agree to work in tandem to take care of five-month-old Steph and the dog, Sammy. Neighbors offer to mow the lawn and take in the mail. Off Steve and Janet drive, first to Long Island, then to Seattle, 3,100 miles with two-year-old Reid in tow.

They arrive Monday morning after 48 hours on the road, apparently unexpected.

"Who's the doctor?" a nurse asks.

"Dr. Gifford," Janet replies.

"Harold Gifford?"

"No, Peter Gifford."

"I'm sure you are mistaken. Dr. Peter Gifford is our department chairman."

"Right. And he's Jan's doctor," Steve interjects, not appreciating the nurse's huffy attitude. "Here's his phone number. You want to call and *check*?"

She calls. Janet is moved to the front of every line.

For the next three months, from May through July, Janet undergoes a barrage of radiation. More, Dr. Gifford admits later, than they have ever given another patient. Her mouth fills with sores, her face scalds crimson. On outings with Steve and Reid to explore the Seattle area, Janet finds herself more and more self-conscious about her face. In a checkout line at Sears—Janet had selected a dress for her brother's wedding—a customer looks at Janet's bright red cheeks, and says, "My God, what were you doing? Lying in the sun?" Janet says, "No. I had radiation." The woman recoils, grimacing, and flees to another checkout line, her own face reddening.

I never have a good comeback, Janet thinks. I wish I could think of something, anything, to say.

5

Alive

Janet

AUGUST 1989

One month later, a muggy August afternoon greets Janet as she slides open the glass door to the screened porch, holding Reid's hand as they descend the wooden steps to the shade of their backyard. How normal this feels, she thinks as she strolls barefoot down the grassy slope to their dock nestled in tall phragmites reeds reverberating with the scratchy whistles of red-winged blackbirds. For three years her feet have trod this hillside, yet now, each day, this act feels brand new, as though life were starting up fresh each morning.

She steps nimbly into their motorboat, the *Seabird*, and Steve hands her baby Steph decked out in a tiny orange life jacket. Reid clambers aboard—he's two now, a big boy—and Sammy, Janet's golden retriever, follows. Steve pushes off and climbs in. Janet takes the wheel and putts them down the creek.

At the first bend, a great-crested flycatcher, his upright gray head complemented by a yellow belly, calls from the tip of a dead branch; his coarse, rising *kreeep* resounding above the quiet drone of the motor. A fish crow flies over, uttering a hoarse *uh-uhn*. Other birdsong seems hushed by the heat, by the weight of the dark green canopy draped over their forested port side. They motor past lawns and docks, the idle boats and modest homes of friends. A lone ring-billed gull glides by.

Under her visor, Janet's reddish-blond hair, curly with humidity, flutters in the breeze she's created. The heaviness of the air vanishes as she steers toward the South River, passing the osprey nest where three fledglings—their feather tips still edged in white, their eyes still orange—pant after a day of learning to catch their own fish. At the mouth of the creek, Janet opens the throttle and roars into the river toward the Chesapeake Bay.

"I'll take your six months, Dr. Brusher. And raise you sixty years!" Janet shouts to the waves.

Laughing with every slam of the hull, she repeats a mantra in her head to the beat: Alive, Alive, Alive. She cheers at the flare of her white foamy wake, grins at Steve, sticks out her tongue at Reid, who sticks his tongue out at her. Throttling down, she steers the boat to a secluded beach. Steve throws the anchor as they coast into the shallows, jumps out, and gathers up the kids. Reid wades to the beach to dig in the sand; Steph, held under her daddy's arm, splashes at the water and giggles.

Janet smiles at Sammy as he paddles after the stick Steve tosses. That dog loves the water as much as I do, she muses, recalling last December when Sammy broke through the ice covering the creek to go swimming.

Last December. Back when her first thought every morning was what day her second baby would be born. Now she wakes and thinks cancer.

But this afternoon, her mind wanders back to childhood days on Long Island, to days of swimming and fishing with her sisters, Lynn and Donna, and boating with Little Grandpa. She leans back in the captain's chair, closes her eyes, and treats her face to the sun's warmth. As a light wind wafts over her, she takes a long deep breath.

I could stay here forever.

6

Back to Seattle

Janet

SEPTEMBER 1989

September rolls in and the late morning air, hanging on to a bit of evening coolness, is rich with cicada song. But all Janet feels are the rivulets of sweat dripping down her back as she sits on the closed cover of the toilet, a coffee mug filled with blood in her hands. What is happening? she thinks. Please, God. Please don't let this be the cancer again. She's never had nosebleeds like this before. And this is the third one in two days.

Steve calls Dr. Gifford in Seattle. Janet, hearing the urgency in his firm voice, grips her hands in her lap to keep them from shaking. After dropping the receiver into its cradle, he strides into the bathroom and sits on the tiled floor. He rests his callused, summer-tanned hand on her knee.

"We've got to go back to Seattle," Steve says, his voice gentle but unflinching. "Dr. Gifford's lab will cover the cost of the flight. He wants us to come out right away."

Janet stares into the eyes she fell in love with nine years ago. "I can't stand this," she chokes. Shoulders slumped, she collapses into Steve's embrace, and they hold each other, sure the tumor has roared back, and this is the end they've each feared.

The nosebleeds remain at bay during their flight to Seattle. But anxiety accompanies them.

After the CT scan, Janet waits with Steve, feeling the weight of his arm around her thin shoulders. Sobs want to arrive, but she checks herself. Not here. Not now. Hold it together.

Two slow hours pass. A fish tank burbles. Janet gazes at a young mother, head resting in her left hand as she rocks a stroller back and forth with her right. A toddler rolls his tiny yellow backhoe up and down her leg. Rhythms of endurance.

"Hey," Steve says. "Let's play what-if." Janet takes a deep breath. What now?

"What if the news is bad?" Steve says. "What are we going to do? Well, we could sell the house, put $100,000 profit in the bank, take the rest, buy a big boat, and sail around the world with the kids and the dog until the money runs out.

"Or, if you're okay, then name one thing, anything, and I will buy it for you. What do you want?"

Janet ponders.

"I want two things," she says, chuckling despite herself. "I want a piano for the living room. And I want a boat that holds the whole family with a cabin just my size."

"Ha!" Steve laughs. "You got it—one piano. And I will build that boat for you."

"How does he do it?" she thinks. "He keeps finding ways to keep me going. But what if he can't this time. What if this is it?"

Staring down the hallway, they sit up straight as Dr. Gifford runs toward them. He charges forward with a euphoric grin that's very unlike him, waving a sheet of paper. To Janet's amazement, he jumps in the air and clicks his heels.

"It's okay, it's okay, it's okay!" Dr. Gifford shouts. "A blood vessel was left too close to the surface after the first surgery. It has absolutely nothing to do with the tumor. You are fine, Janet, you're fine!"

Brought from deepest low to this sudden high, Janet is stunned into uncontrollable laughter, the news almost too good to believe, too unexpected to bear. She bursts from her chair to hug Dr. Gifford, then Steve, her laughter and tears intermingling.

"You know," Steve says to her later as they walk holding hands toward the exit. "We have a problem."

"I know," Janet says, her voice shaky with relief and exhaustion.

"We came up with these cool things to do, and you got a new lease on life. Who wants to go back to the old grind? Let's do it all anyway."

At the hotel, they shower to remove all traces of hospital funk, change into fresh clothes—clean jeans, a sleeveless white button-down blouse dotted with tiny flowers for Janet, a blue polo for Steve—then head out to a favorite Italian restaurant they found when they were in Seattle earlier in the summer. Grinning at each other over linguini and clams, they try to set this new reality firmly into the framework of their lives. They pick up a bottle of cheap champagne after dinner, then in their hotel room, with exultant cheers, Janet clinks glasses with Steve, over and over again.

7

Birthday Surprise

Janet

April 1992

Janet pulls a crispy-skinned chicken from the oven and sets it aside to rest. It's been three years since the cancer diagnosis and palate surgery, three years since radiation in Seattle, and she revels in daily life, in taking care of the kids, in cooking. Whenever she smells the rich odor of roast chicken, she imagines her family's voices, their exhortations of delight when they taste their favorite meal. "Eat well," she whispers to the Carolina chickadee at the feeder outside the kitchen window. The gray crest on the tufted titmouse seems extra bushy today, the green fuzz of new spring leaves more vibrant. She rummages through the utensil drawer, vowing once again to organize it, finds the masher and is draining the potatoes when she hears Steve come in the front door. "Hey Sammy, good boy," he says. He sweeps into the kitchen, gives Janet a kiss, and hands her a note.

She can tell by his face that something is up. "What's this?" Giggling with a schoolgirl's giddiness, she unfolds the lined piece of paper and reads the list: flip-flops, bathing suit, visor, sunscreen. "Steve, what is this?"

"It's your packing list," Steve says, giving her a bear hug. "Tomorrow, I am taking you on a trip to the Florida Keys for your birthday."

"Oh, Steve, you're kidding. You are kidding, right? Wait...oh Steve, I get it now, but wait...where is it?"

"Where's what?" Steve asks, shaking his head as Janet darts around the family room, looking at the ceiling and behind the television. "And what are you doing?"

"Looking for Allen Funt's camera," she says, checking behind one couch pillow, then another. "Am I on Candid Camera?"

"Are you kidding? No, this is real. I am taking you to Florida. I've got our moms all lined up to watch the kids. We're going. Surprise!"

"I can't believe it. I just can't believe it." All through dinner, as she slices through a piece of chicken breast, lifts a forkful of hot buttery mashed potatoes, and scoops up peas from the pool of gravy, Janet laughs in wonder. In the evening, she feels the thrill of anticipation bubbling through her as she packs up everything on Steve's list, plus a few items he forgot. They're going to the Florida Keys.

No itinerary, no expectations, they drive, stopping when they are intrigued or tired. This beach to swim and snorkel; this one to surfcast for fish; this one for a picnic and a walk. The first couple days on the Keys are glorious, but the sun and salt air work on Janet in a reverse alchemic twist. Everything good turns sour. Uncharacteristically cranky, Janet grumbles about Steve's daily plans. In a last-ditch effort to please, Steve splurges on a fancy seafood restaurant overlooking Islamorada.

The waiter seats them near a large window, drapes white linen napkins over their laps, pours ice water into glasses etched with dolphins, asks if they'd like to see the wine list.

Janet twists away and stares at a line of brown pelicans swooping toward the sea, rising in unison as though tethered one to the next; at the turquoise water becoming indigo as the sun dips low; at the silhouettes of egrets coming in to roost for the night; at palm leaves hanging limply against the orange and pink sky.

None of it matters. She turns her hard stare on Steve.

"You can tell me why you brought me on this trip. What are you waiting to tell me?" she says, her voice as firm as her rigid body.

"What's that?"

"You brought me on this trip to tell me that I'm going to die."

"Jan! What in the world makes you think that?"

"There's no other reason you would have brought me on this trip."

"What about I love you and wanted to surprise you?"

"No, that can't be it."

"Aaaaa!" Steve tosses his napkin onto the floor and throws up his arms. "Fine. Alright—yes, you're right, you're going to die."

"I knew it. Tell me," Janet says. She thought she was prepared for this pronouncement, but instead, feels her stomach plummet, her body shrink into itself.

Steve leans toward her, his hands gripping the edges of the table, his eyes wild. "You are going to die because I am going to drag you out by the scruff of your neck and hold you under the water in the bay until you are dead because you've ruined my trip, you creep."

"What!" Janet tips back in shock. She takes in and releases a deep breath—the breath she realizes she's been holding all week. The sensation reminds her of childhood when she would stand in the kitchen doorway and push her arms as hard as she could against the doorframe for one minute, so when she stepped away, her arms would rise, unbidden, toward the ceiling. Like an angel. That is the feeling entering her whole body, a lightness she hasn't felt for weeks, or has it been months? Or years? She feels invincible, unsinkable, a true Molly Brown.

Even when life tosses icebergs in her way.

Near the middle of the second week, their money runs low. They find an ad for a motel room, only $16 a night. Thrilled, they book it. They're even more excited when the address leads them to the water. Their "motel room" is a fifty-foot long by twenty-foot wide houseboat, half sunk. A pelican stands on its bow. When they lie on the narrow bed to test it out, Janet chortles; she can't stop rolling onto Steve. A three-bladed fan with only two blades emits a strange humming sound. One dim light bulb casts a mysterious shadow.

"Steve, this is perfect! We have to give it a name. Let's call it The Enchanted Palace."

Two days later, they head north toward Annapolis, but run out of gas on I-95 at 2 a.m. Every protective hair on Steve's arms rises; he'd heard on the radio there've been sniper shootings in the area. But when the driver of an 18-wheeler stops to offer them a lift to the next gas station, Janet jumps at the chance. She bounces on the seat between Steve and the driver. "I can't believe I'm riding in an 18-wheeler. This is so cool!"

The next day they pull into their favorite vacation spot on the Outer Banks. Planning to fish all day, they barely get their lines in the water when a violent storm kicks up, sending waves crashing and Steve and Janet heading home. Tucked beside the luggage on the back floor, a dish of seawater holds hermit crabs they've collected as a present for Stephanie and Reid.

Driving slowly in the pouring rain, windshield wipers struggling to keep up, they hit a pothole. The dish overturns. Hermit crabs scuttle everywhere.

Steve pulls over to collect them. Soaked in seconds as he gets out to reach under the backseats, he plucks one after another from their hiding places. Janet laughs and laughs, a catharsis spreading through her like sunrise. "C'mon, let's go."

"No. I am going to find them all. They'll get lost and die and stink up the car."

When they finally get underway again, Janet rests her head and closes her eyes. She remembers that first week, when one thought ate at her belly, turning every moment bitter: I'm dying. This is my last meal. This is my last Tuesday. Then Steve yelled at her at that seafood restaurant: "Damn it, I love you, can't you believe that?" She smiles, recalling the wild frustration on his face, her sudden realization she really was okay. Rain drums on the roof of the car, the wipers swipe a rhythmic beat. Her shoulders relax as she nods toward sleep.

8

Upper Darby, Pennsylvania

Dotty

MAY 1992

I reach up and grasp another clothespin between my thumb and forefinger, savoring the texture of the smooth wooden surface. How many times have I done this, I think, as I pinch and squeeze one after the other, working my way down the clothesline removing cloth diapers, small dresses, and my husband Jonathan's colorful shirts, folding each one into the wicker basket.

The air is warm this spring afternoon, T-shirt weather, the sun just resting in the tops of the sycamores lining the street. "It's a good drying day," I say to myself, repeating the phrase my mother always said on sunny days like this when my twin sister Patty and I hung up clothes with her in our backyard, the wide expanse of grass dewy with morning, our bare feet wet and covered in cut grass from Dad's mowing. I've put up a clothesline everywhere I've lived, bringing in fresh air with the laundry.

The SEPTA subway train squeals as it turns at the end of the line three blocks away at 69th Street station. House sparrows *chirr-upp* while searching for seeds in the gutters; starlings squabble on nearby roofs. Once again I wish we lived where native birds were more plentiful. Last spring, an oriole appeared, and I hope one will again this year. Oh, I know there are good birds out in the parks and woodlands, but getting there seems like too much work. Maybe this weekend we could go for a walk at Tinicum, at the John Heinz National Wildlife Refuge, and look for migrants. But I don't know. I guess I'm just tired.

"Mommy," four-year-old Ruth says, "when will Daddy be home?"

"Daddy!" Helen chirps.

"Soon. He called from work about twenty minutes ago. He's on the subway now and should be coming up the sidewalk soon."

Helen leaps from the sandbox Jonathan built on the concrete half of our tiny side yard and rushes on toddler legs to the steps leading to the sidewalk. She plunks down, ready to wait.

"Hi, Bud!" she yells, waving and jumping up as she sees our neighbor ambling up the road. A Navy veteran and retired bulldozer operator for PECO's coal division, Bud makes the rounds of the neighborhood each day, greeting friends, checking in, offering help. His ability to fix anything has saved us over and over—from replacing the brakes on our

'66 Chevy Malibu station wagon to helping Jonathan put a new kitchen in our duplex.

"Hi, Peanut," Bud says, coming over to give her bare leg a squeeze. "Hi, Ruth. Hi, Dotty."

Helen reaches to give him a hug. "Say hi to Mary for me," Ruth adds from the sandbox.

Bud and Mary are like surrogate grandparents for our daughters, their own grandparents far away—an eight-hour drive to my parents in South Dartmouth, Massachusetts, in the southeastern part of the state where I grew up; a six-hour drive to Jonathan's parents in Ithaca, NY. We visit both sets of grandparents regularly but having Bud and Mary across the street fuels the girls' need for constant contact. And their two daughters, Maureen and Janet, have their parents' charm, babysitting for Ruth and Helen when we need a night out.

We might never have met them.

Jonathan and I moved here seven years ago from Sandy Spring, Maryland. I had been teaching high school science and coaching lacrosse at Sandy Spring Friends School; he'd been hunting for a job but found no prospects. Realizing he needed a master's degree, Jonathan opted for graduate work in regional planning at the University of Pennsylvania in Philadelphia. I got a job teaching biology and coaching field hockey, basketball, and lacrosse at another Quaker school, Friends Central.

Looking for an inexpensive place to rent, we met with an agent at her real estate office. We asked her about Upper Darby, which seemed the perfect locale—close enough for me to bike to Friends Central and for Jonathan to walk to the subway headed downtown each day. But she shook her head, grimacing. "Oh, no," she said, then whispered behind her hand, "blue-collar." Jonathan and I glanced at each other. "Show us what's listed there." We found our home on Ashby Road.

These memories flow in as I cuddle next to Helen on the steps waiting for Jonathan. It's had its downsides—grueling muggy heat in the summer; a neighbor across the alley whose shouting at his mother brings the police; another neighbor who leaves his large dogs indoors to bark all day. And it's city; concrete everywhere. The metallic grinding screech of the subway wakes me each morning.

But the plusses have worked for us. We've created a small garden in our side yard for tomatoes and herbs, and we can walk to the grocery store, the library, and Sears. Close friends from college—some also work at Friends Central—live nearby. We love the diversity. Ruth goes to a Jewish preschool, both girls go to a Black Muslim daycare while I coach, and we all attend Quaker meeting on Sunday. Bud and Mary are Catholic, and Ruth especially loves when Mary takes her and Helen to see the big crèche outside her church during Advent. Every Christmas, the girls get a new ornament for the tree, and last year, Ruth's was a blue blown-glass Madonna and baby Jesus. She hung it in a prominent place on the front of our jack pine tree, a misshapen Charlie Brown tree with a few dozen ornaments.

"Daddy!" Helen careens down the sidewalk when she spots him. Ruth follows. Together they wrap their arms around Jonathan's legs and sit on his feet. He laughs trying to walk as they hang on tight. "Gee," he calls up to me. "I must be extra tired today. My legs feel so heavy."

The girls giggle, letting go only so he can climb up the steps. They grab his hands to show him their creation in the sandbox. "Look, Daddy, this is Upper Darby," Ruth informs him, pointing out her preschool and friends' houses. "And here's the library filled with *Curious George* books."

Jonathan lies down on the warm concrete beside them, stretching out his legs and loosening his tie. They sit on his stomach and chat away.

Since graduate school, Jonathan has been working for the National Park Service's Mid-Atlantic Regional Office, most recently as a branch chief in park planning. But we've both been hoping for a change—he for a different job, me for a new locale. Two weeks ago, when he told me he was offered a job as director of the Columbia River Gorge Commission in the small town of White Salmon, Washington, I jumped at the chance to get out of the city. "Take it!" I'd said, leaping off the couch to hug him. "Say yes! Right now! I'll start packing."

Leaving them all outside to play, I start supper, drizzling lemon juice, olive oil, and oregano over

chicken parts to bake and eat with cinnamon-sprin-
kled rice. Then the burning sensation in my lower
gut kicks in. I eat a few crackers, hoping to ease
the pain, now too familiar. The oven preheats, I rub
my low belly, the burn getting more intense. Ugh,
I think. What is this?

9

Gut Feeling

Dotty

OCTOBER 1994

Toss, step, hit. Toss, step, hit. I serve over and over to my eighth-grade volleyball team, trying to get them to move their feet.

"C'mon, c'mon! Okay, good job. Next. C'mon...ahh, hustle, get the ball."

For forty minutes, I serve like a machine.

"Bump...yes...set...good! Ahh, c'mon now, where's the spike?"

The searing pain in my back flares, untouched by the neoprene brace I wear pretending it will help. My intestines feel as though they've been doused in acid.

Toss, step, hit. Toss, step, hit.

Though saddened to say goodbye to Bud and Mary and so many Upper Darby friends two years ago, I was thrilled to come out to this small town of White Salmon, Washington, perched above the Columbia River Gorge. The girls here had never seen a field hockey game, had never heard of lacrosse, but they needed a middle school coach for their interscholastic volleyball and basketball teams. As a multi-sport jock in high school and college, plus a varsity-level coach for eleven years, I knew I could handle it. And I had handled it...up until now.

After scrimmages and wind sprints, practice ends, and I call the two eighth-grade captains into my office.

"What's up?" I ask. "Why's everybody so off today?"

They shrug, glance at each other, look down at their laps. "I dunno," they echo.

"Okay. Fine. I will see you tomorrow." I remain at my desk until all the girls have left the locker room, exhaustion pinning me to my chair. Our season's almost over, five more days, we're undefeated, one more big game. What is going on?

The truth dawns as though through thick fog. The girls recognized it before I did. Nothing's wrong with them. It's me. Embarrassment at my maniacal serving-machine demonstration hits me like a gut punch, and I acknowledge it as a last desperate attempt to prove to myself I could handle whatever is expected of me. To prove to myself, as I've been trying to do for the past two years, I can ignore ferocious pain and just keep going. But the claws have sunk deep.

Dragging myself to standing, I shuffle into the gym and turn off the breaker panel's row of lights. In darkness penetrated only by the glow of exit signs, I gaze across the wide expanse of floor, then bend over, hands on knees, trying to catch my breath. If I collapse, when will someone find me.

I make it to my car, drive past the llama farm and the quiet cherry orchards to slump onto the couch.

"You're done," Jonathan says in a gentle voice, putting his arm around me. And I know it, we both have known it for weeks, the pain dogging me, increasing in intensity day after day accompanied by unrelenting fatigue, but I couldn't say no to my team. Ruth and Helen have seen me lie on the couch before, when the pain and exhaustion prevailed over my desire to play with them. Six-year old Ruth gives me a hug and says, "We'll take care of you, Mommy." Helen, now four, cuddles up and kisses me over and over.

Stoicism runs in my family. I saw it in Grandpa when my mother's parents lived up the road. My grandmother found him crawling upstairs to go to bed after his appendix had burst. My admiration for my played-college-football-without-helmets grandfather led me down a similar path. I've regularly forced myself beyond normal limits: pulled so many all-nighters during my freshman year in college I only slept a total ten hours a week; ran wind sprints to "cure" menstrual cramps; carried not only my overloaded backpack but shuttled it with the backpack of a sick student from the bottom of the Grand Canyon to the rim despite agonizing pain in knees and hips. Worked a gardening job while pregnant until my back pain got so bad I barely slept for two weeks; returned to coaching high school basketball one week after giving birth, Ruth strapped to my chest. *I can do it* has been my rallying cry. *I can do it all. And I will not complain.*

This time, I listened. Stopped. Doesn't feel right, yet I know it is. Now what?

When Ruth was born, our acupuncturist introduced us to Angel Cards, a set of small rectangular cards, silver faced with the outline of an angel, white with a single word on the back. Offering the fifty cards silver-side up to her toddler son, she asked him to pick one for baby Ruth, to be her birth angel to guide her through life. He pondered and chose. Purpose. Two-year-old Ruth chose Helen's birth angel: Joy. Both were fitting prophecies.

Reconciled, gut burning, I sneak out of bed that night and lay out the angel cards face down in a messy pile—not in a pretty shape like I often design for Ruth and Helen—and let my eyes skim them, waiting for one to say *pick me.* A thought niggles at the back of my brain—what if I select the wrong one? What if I only think it's the right one?

Closing my eyes to breathe and center, I look again and find one that beckons. Beauty. I smile, having chosen this many times. Beauty is what keeps me going: the backyard birds, the wildflowers on Mt. Adams, the view down the gorge, the way the mountain ridges take on multiple shades of blue as the sun sets.

Another one: Responsibility. Seriously? Don't I have enough of that with the girls, the house, the yard, the bills...oh. Maybe it means being more mindful of taking care of me. I'm not so good at that.

Two more: Harmony. Simplicity. Perhaps if I allow myself to rest, and simplify my life, I will achieve more balance and harmony. A lovely thought, but how am I supposed to get anything done?

I've undergone so many tests; all negative. Seen so many doctors; one GI doctor kind enough to say he knew the pain wasn't all in my head but had no answers. I appreciated his honesty.

Back in bed, I try another of my latest pain management devices. Imagery. Skeptical to say the least, I've been surprised by its effectiveness. Each time, my internal journey returns me to Havasu Falls.

I visited this stunning isolated place while a naturalist at the Grand Canyon. After three days patrolling a remote trail descending from the North Rim to the Colorado River, my co-worker and I joined a raft of rangers. We went ashore at the Havasupai reservation and trekked into the town of Supai. After downing the ranger-lauded "best chocolate milkshakes ever," we hiked to Havasu Falls.

Now under flannel sheets with Jonathan breathing quietly beside me, I close my eyes and imagine descending rock steps hewn from the ruddy Redwall Limestone. Ten, nine, eight...with each step down, I envision less pain. When I reach the bottom, a Costa's hummingbird greets me, flashing his purple head and long flare of throat feathers, like one did when I visited sixteen years ago, intrigued by my bright orange backpack. I walk past a green-stemmed paloverde tree, past travertine-encrusted turquoise pools, and arrive at an imaginary large black boulder smoothed by the river and warmed by the sun. Nestling into a groove that fits my body, I gaze into the pool where the silent Havasu waterfall ends. Now to focus on the pain.

Once, I visualized my pain as a rusty rake scraping its sharp tines across my back. When I asked for a healer, the rake turned into warm silver balls that rolled and mended the shredded muscles. Tonight, the pain appears as big globs of brown mud that stick to my abdominal cavity and pulse like bubbling lava. I ask for help.

Who should arise but the cartoon figure, Casper the Friendly Ghost, scooting in with a big smile, scaring the gloppy mud-monster (as the lava turned into) until it shrank, turned white, and became part of Casper.

After resting on the warm boulder for a moment, I jump off and breathe-count myself back up the steps. The pain has dulled. I turn over to sleep.

10

Dogs and Family

Janet

April 1995

Sitting on the floor of the Kitty Hawk pet shop, six years after hearing she had six months to live, Janet finds she can forget sometimes. Forget the tumor lurking in her skull is hard to kill. That even though the doctors are optimistic, questions linger. How long will the cancer remain dormant? What's coming next? How much time has she got? Her rigid jaw reminds her. The obturator she wears— the prostheses to cover the hole in the roof of her mouth—reminds her.

But what joy when she forgets. Right now, a puppy wriggles under her fingers, licks her palm. She can't stop patting the tawny head. A missing bit of fur adds to his comical look.

"You should get him!" her sister says.

"Lynn," Janet says, "we really don't need a second dog in the house."

"Sure you do!"

"Mom, he's so cute," Steph and Reid chorus. "You'll love him."

The others wander off to roam the pet shop she and Lynn discovered while visiting their mother at her vacation condo. Janet sits cross-legged and snuggles the golden retriever puppy in her lap, remembering Sammy at this age—a fuzzy golden retriever-terrier bundle she fell in love with when she was twenty. He was devoted to her, never wanting them to be parted. If she went out with her sisters to the local bar to laugh and tell stories until midnight—her mother's curfew for them—she would often come home to find Sammy had peed in her shoes.

Oh, Sammy. You always watched out for me. I never thought I could get another dog after you. Can it really be two years now? You were my buddy for twenty years, almost half my life. I could tell you anything.

She thought her heart would never recover, but she missed having a dog around. Seven months after Sammy died, she'd relented, and she and Steve got a mixed-breed puppy—part German Shepard, part Bernese Mountain Dog—from the SPCA. Steve wanted to name the fluffy brown ball Bear but got outvoted by the rest of the family who preferred the name he came with: Woody because he was found in the woods. Like Sammy, Woody became her dog.

Janet still feels pangs of sorrow about leaving Sammy behind with her mother during those five years of travel around Europe. She'd quit her job at the bakery after graduating from high school and begun working at the IRS with her mother.

She'd reluctantly gone to community college for two years—an eternity, but her mother had insisted—studying anthropology and earning her associate degree. But she wanted to travel. For five glorious years, she explored Italy, Spain, England. The thrill she got from seeing the Colosseum and Stonehenge remains. She wishes she could do it all again.

When she'd come back from her travels, Sammy would put his paws on her shoulders, lick her face, and leap around her legs yipping; finally at ease when she returned to live at home. With her aptitude for languages, she'd hoped to work at the United Nations, but they required a precision she lacked and a higher degree.

Scratching the puppy's belly, she recalls her forays into graduate school. She'd always loved math and decided to pursue it but found one class to be quite a shock. When her advisor recommended she take economics, she thought he meant home economics. She laughs, shaking her head. What a ditz I was.

Along with her associate degree, she needed three more years in the graduate program at the University of New York at Stony Brook to get simultaneous bachelor's and master's degrees. Those three years had a rocky start.

Those tests, she thinks. I always felt so dumb. In one math course, Janet would answer the few questions she knew, then hand in the test. She'd be the first one out the door.

She loves Steve's story about noticing her. He'd been in that same class and couldn't take his eyes off her, marveling at how fast she could finish the tests. Wow, brains and beauty, he'd thought. Pretty cool. He'd asked a friend if she knew her.

"Yeah, sure I know her," his friend said, nodding. "Janet's my roommate."

"So, what's the gig? Does she have a boyfriend?"

"Yeah, she's got a boyfriend, but he's a jerk. So, if you want to run him off that would be just fine. I'm having a surprise birthday party for her next week. You should come."

When Janet arrived at the party, her boyfriend drunk and hanging all over her, Steve set about intimidating him. Tall, smart, funny, sober Steve won her heart, and that evening she agreed to a real date, followed by many more.

When Steve found out she was struggling in her studies, he tutored her. Ha! she remembers. I got A's and he was getting B's. The tutoring stopped but the romance continued, even when she moved to D.C. for an IRS summer internship, then accepted the offer of a full-time job. She enrolled at George Washington University to continue her studies.

I don't know how I did it. When did I eat? When did I sleep? I ran from class to class, sprinting through the cafeteria to eat a lemon for lunch. So much energy!

A year and a half later, in October 1981, she and Steve got engaged. In September 1982, Sammy joined them in their Long Island wedding and on their Outer

Banks honeymoon. Protective Sammy growled at any man who came near Janet, but he'd approved of Steve from the start.

Lynn returns to where Janet is sitting.

"Well, are you going to get him? He sure seems to like you."

"I just love him," Janet replies, nuzzling the puppy's head, "but I'll have to think about it."

Back at the condo, she calls Steve at work. "Are you crazy?" he says. "Woody is only a year-and-a-half old and already eighty pounds. We need another dog like a hole in the head."

At the end of the week, before she and Lynn leave the Outer Banks with the kids, Janet returns to the pet shop. Two golden retriever puppies are left, including the one with the little tuft of fur missing on the top of his head. Janet cuddles him into her arms and names him Dan. Two dogs, two kids. Just right.

Janet and Steve

11

Family Matters

Janet

JULY 1995

"Quit shoving."

"You quit shoving."

"Move over!"

"Mom!"

"Shh, shh, shh," Janet says, closing Stephanie and Reid, all elbows and knees, into the large cardboard box, smoothing and taping the wrapping paper over the sides and top, then sticking on a giant blue bow. "Grandma will be here any minute."

"Shh"

"Be quiet!"

"I am being quiet."

"Move over."

"You move over."

"Mom, is she here yet?"

Janet shushes them again, then hides around the corner from her parents' back door, smiling as she watches the box shake. How did they get so big?

Six and eight and so much themselves. She enjoys Stephanie's inquisitive nature and shares her love of nature and animals; feels deep pride watching Reid help his dad build and repair things.

The box wobbles. "Reid, get your elbow out of my face."

Janet gazes over the tree-lined East Islip backyard where she grew up. She knows every inch. The blue and white Madonna resides in the shrine her father made in the middle of the four birch trunks; the pink rose bush blooms. A robin searches the lawn, head cocked to the side, listening. A catbird mewls from the rose bush.

Today the always-immaculate lawn is festooned with lawn chairs, a couple of umbrellas for shade, a kiddie pool. She ticks off the decorations and refreshments. Party banner strung between the trees: check. Tablecloth, napkins, Chinet plates, plastic cups, plastic utensils: check. Lasagna, meatballs, sauce, barbequed chicken legs, pasta salad, chips, beer, check. Lemonade: check. Birthday cake: check.

Scuffling sounds come from inside the box. Like a bushel of brawling crabs.

Dad's garden looks good this year, she muses, watching him check the tomatoes for hornworms. But she has not inherited her Dad's green thumb. She's tried to grow tomatoes, flowers. But nothing ever survives.

Nicknamed Zucchini Grandpa, Janet's dad had also kept ducks and geese and chickens to feed his young family, and he hunted and fished. Weekdays, he commuted from Long Island into the city to work as a CPA on Wall Street, but on weekends and summer evenings, he sold concessions and took tickets at the Islip Speedway. As a child, Janet loved the track, her face pressed against the chain-link fence, the smell of fuel and burnt tires, the heat shimmering over the asphalt, the race cars all blur and roar.

"Ugh, Steph, quit pinching." More shuffling.

Those childhood summers. The chore of picking endless tomatoes, ears of corn, cucumbers, and zucchini with her sisters, Lynn, one year older, and Donna, one year younger. David and CJ came later. The sisters were in middle school when the boys were born, graduating high school while they were negotiating elementary school. Now everyone is grown.

Donna's car pulls in, she and her mom chatting as they head inside. "Shh! Grandma's coming," Janet whisper-shouts. The box goes still.

I can't wait to see her face, Janet thinks, shivering in anticipation. Her mom, making sure her five children got the good pieces of meat, even if it meant she got the gristly end piece; making every holiday a family event. But she'd always downplayed her own birthday. "Don't go to any trouble for me," she'd say.

Ha! That's why we're having this party in July, instead of back at your birthday in March. We'll get you now.

Donna ushers her mother, Doris, down the back steps. "Mom, there's a big box. What do you think that is?"

"Oh, for heaven's sake, what is this? Did you do this, Donna?"

"Not me. I don't know what it is."

"Well, who put up all these decorations? Donna, what is going on?"

"I dunno, Mom, but you better open that box."

Doris steps over to the box, her wavy shoulder-length brown hair blowing in the breeze. She pulls off the bow, peels off the tape, and—as she opens the flaps—out pop Steph and Reid.

"Oh my! Stephanie! Reid! What are you doing here? My goodness, what is all this?"

"It's a party for you, Grandma!"

"Happy Birthday!"

"But it isn't my birthday. My birthday's in March."

"We know! We wanted to surprise you."

"Oh, and look. Janet! Well everyone is here, aren't they. Oh my."

Family pours through the back door, thrilled the surprise has worked. Doris scurries to a nearby chair, and Janet plunks beside her to give her a hug.

"I just can't believe this, Janet. Did you girls do all this?"

"It's all for you, Mom. You deserve it."

Like her husband, Doris has held several jobs. Besides raising five children, she worked at the

IRS, typed and read letters for a blind man, plus volunteered at church.

Janet looks at her mother's face, at her ever-present smile, and sees weariness under the delight. When did she get old?

Lynn, the daughter living at home, knows the weariness began seventeen years before. Doris was forty-nine when she was diagnosed with cervical cancer. She'd told no one, just cooked and froze meals until Lynn asked what she was doing. When she went in for surgery, and later for treatments, Doris insisted on going alone. "No one needs to come with me," she'd said.

Steph bounces over from the pool, dripping in her pink bathing suit. "Can we eat now?" she asks.

"Yes, let's eat," Janet laughs.

"C'mon, Grandma," Steph says, tugging on Doris's hand. "You have to go first."

"You're the boss," her grandmother says, saluting. "Let's go!"

Plates and cups fill with the bounty. Janet longs for barbeque chicken and corn chips but chooses the softest foods, hoping her rigid jaw and few remaining teeth can mush it down. Four years ago, surgeons attempted a z-plasty, trying to stretch her atrophied jaw muscle to allow more flexibility, but it didn't work. Now, even with family, she feels embarrassed: her cheek scarred, her mouth twisted upward. The food she eats can get caught under her obturator or go up her nose.

Ten years into the future she'll think, If I'd known back then how I would look now, I wouldn't have been so self-conscious.

Today, for her mother's party, Janet sets discomfort aside and celebrates. She fills her plate and eats what she can, letting fun prevail.

12

Home in Annapolis

Janet

OCTOBER 1995

Janet sets the oven to 450 degrees and selects a chef's knife for the annual October demolition. She cuts a wide circle around the scratchy stem, yanks off the orange top, then with a large metal spoon, scrapes around and around the inside of yet another pumpkin from the farm.

I liked the hayride best, she thinks as she plops the stringy mass of seeds onto the newspapered counter. But she also loves the yearly banter between Steph and Reid over what constitutes the best pumpkin for a jack-o'-lantern, their eyes bright, their cheeks red in air so cool and fresh it feels like diving into the ocean. She and Steve had helped them clean out and carve their pumpkins, but today, while they're at school, it's time to prepare a medium-sized sugar pumpkin for pie, a bowling-ball-sized one for the head of her scarecrow that sags by the front door, wads of rags shoved into Steve's old jeans and flannel shirt.

Janet laughs, knowing her family thinks she's a bit goofy, but she loves holidays and looks forward to decorating just as she and her mother did.

She cleans out the larger pumpkin, sets it aside to carve the face later, then cuts the sugar pumpkin into quarters and scoops out the seeds to reveal the reddish-orange pulp. When the oven dings, she places the quarters onto an oiled pan, pops them in to roast, and sets the timer.

In the family room, she permits herself time to rest on the couch and pats the dogs lolling around her legs. Tonight there'll be a planning session with the kids about how to make this year's Halloween costumes; Steph wants to be a cat, Reid, anything gory with blood. Baskets overflowing with amber and crimson leaves she's collected festoon tables and the floor, reminding her of earlier days.

When she and Steve were paying off their college loans and working at low-level IRS jobs, they lived in three apartments, a different one each year at the same condo complex in Largo, Maryland. With no budget for decor, she'd adorned the window sills with fall leaves, propped dried flowers in drinking glasses.

Ruffling Dan's ears, she notices the missing tuft of fur has filled in, though, at seven months, he's not yet fully grown. She fingers the scars on her left cheek, her tongue exploring the edges of her obturator. Exhaustion creeps in, and worry. Even though last week's scan showed her cancer as stable, she knows that means for now. The what ifs, what's nexts, and if onlys niggle at her brain. I just want to keep going for Steph, for Reid. My mother was always there for me and my sisters and brothers. I want to do the same. But she knows this cancer rarely stays quiet. It comes back to haunt.

Her mind wanders to last summer, to their family vacation trip to Acadia National Park in Maine. The jeep broke down three times, but the kindness of strangers plus Steve's ingenuity got them on the road again. Finding a tire to replace a flat in the middle of nowhere eastern Connecticut; Steve fixing a hole in the radiator when they arrived in Maine. That Sunday evening, they went out for ice cream. When they got back to their car in downtown Southwest Harbor, it wouldn't start.

The woman whose house they were renting felt so bad for them she called her nephew who owned the auto parts store in town. "Listen, you need to come down to your shop. I've got people here who need help." Steve walked in, nephew said, "Whatdya need?" Steve said, "There's something wrong with the ignition system on the truck. Can I buy all the possible parts, use the ones I need, and return the rest?" "Absolutely." Steve fixed the ignition with the first part he tried, tourists gawking.

Her favorite memory from Acadia was the joy on Reid's face as he stood at Thunder Hole. All four of them had tromped down the steps from the road, onto the dark cliffs jutting into the ocean. They'd made sure to arrive at high tide—the best time to get wet, Steve had assured Reid. Now the four of them held onto the guard rails, waiting, feeling the cold air rise from the crash of water below. Reid bounced up and down. "C'mon, waves! Come and get me!" Small swells coursed up the narrow slot between the granite cliffs, white foam swirling and roiling. Then their heartbeats sped up. They'd spotted the big wave they'd been anticipating, one they felt sure would result in the famous Thunder Hole upsurge: a massive spray that would deluge them in frigid water as it exploded into the sea cave below with the thunderous boom that gives the site its name. The glee of expectation on Reid's seven-year-old face was as much fun to watch as the inevitable and glorious dousing.

Janet lets out a sigh. Her current sense of waiting feels as though she's anticipating that surge of ice water but without the joy, as though she's standing alone on those granite cliffs on a gray winter day, the wind shrieking. When, she muses, will I be doused?

13

Doused

Janet

DECEMBER 1996

The following year, in late December, Janet waves goodbye as Lynn heads off to roam San Antonio's Riverwalk with Steph sporting her new cowboy hat from Christmas. When Donna and her husband Bob visited earlier, Janet insisted on shopping with them for her children despite her self-consciousness. Steve and Reid are also off exploring, though she can't remember where. Wistful for their adventures, she's more grateful for the reprieve. She needs time to digest the recent news.

She stands at the door of the tiny rented apartment, enjoying the fresh air. In the live oak across the street, a flock of great-tailed grackles bluster and fuss with their high squeals and scratchy chatter. Like radio static. Just what I need, she thinks. More static in my life. Then, a mockingbird, perched on the telephone pole, lets loose with a winding chorus of his best impersonations: robin, cardinal, Carolina wren. Songs that remind her of Maryland, of home.

Janet shuts the door and plunks into an armchair, folding her knees to her chest, arms hugging herself to herself. She still can feel the aftershocks of panic that shook her three months ago when she went for a routine annual scan. The tumors were back, this time on the sheath of her left optic nerve.

Adenoid cystic carcinoma tumors are hard tumors, encased in protective shells or cysts. Soft tumors, like squamous cell tumors, do not have this protective coating. Soft tumors grow fast and die fast. Adenoid cystic carcinoma tumors grow slowly, but insidiously. They are almost impossible to kill.

With the return of Janet's cancer, Steve redoubled his research. He not only found the University of Texas Health Science Center at San Antonio to be the best radiation hope, but he also conferred with the director of radiation oncology, who supported and encouraged Steve's own nascent hypotheses for retarding tumor growth.

San Antonio's state-of-the-art radiation would focus precise beams on the sheath of Janet's optic nerve. Improved since Seattle, this radiation wouldn't scatter and damage surrounding tissue. Her optic nerve would remain untouched and so would her sight.

Two quarter-inch-high studs had been inserted into her skull, four inches apart on the crown of her head. They hadn't hurt going in, but Janet has not forgotten the quick shock of pain she received when she accidentally knocked one on the car door frame.

At the radiation lab, an H-shaped cradle locked onto the studs and secured her head to the table. For an hour, the radiation beams hit the tumors and nothing else.

Janet probes the studs with her index finger. A slight grin belies her experience of sneezing while anchored to the table. I almost snapped my neck!

Ever since October, Steve, his mom and dad, plus Janet's sisters and mom, have all taken turns, either in Annapolis with the kids or in San Antonio with Janet. It's worked, the kids not missing much school, but Woody's been inconsolable. Though Janet feels her longing for Woody as well, a recent phone conversation with Steve when he was back home in Annapolis still makes her laugh.

"I get home from work and Woody's eaten the couch," Steve told her.

"What!"

"Yep, shredded the seat cushions, stuffing every-where. And the wooden armrests? Torn completely off. Let me tell you, for the foreseeable future, that dog is banished to the porch."

Janet uncurls her body and pats her knee. "C'mere, Cleo." Up jumps the stray kitten she found a month ago and couldn't resist. Cleo, for Cleopatra, settles on her lap, purring as Janet strokes her tiger-striped head, scratches her silky white throat. The kitten isn't Woody, but she's offered good comfort. Janet gazes at the flat woven Christmas tree hanging on the wall—Lynn got it for her, plus one for herself—a substitute when they knew they couldn't squeeze a fir tree plus the whole family into the small apartment for Christmas.

Now it's over. In too many ways. They've learned the radiation has failed.

The doctors found recurrence of the cancer at the base of her skull, inside the margins of the area radiated in Seattle. That area cannot be treated again. The Seattle radiation was so powerful it constituted Janet's lifetime dose. Another dose to that area, and bone and tissue would decay. The infected tissue would have to be removed, leaving nothing—no muscle, no bone—to support her skull. She would die. They cannot re-treat that original area.

I just don't know what options I have left, Janet thinks, pulling the kitten close.

14

Seeking Relief

Dotty

DECEMBER 1996

My pain drifts as diffuse as mist; I cannot say here it is. My intestines burn like red-hot coals; my low back sears. If I were a steak, I would be charred.

My new Chinese acupuncturist-herbalist strives to solve the pain mystery. The needles she leaves in my legs and arms "sing" to each other, a vibratory sensation I hope means they're working. She sends me home with a brown paper bag filled with bark, roots, sticks, and who knows what.

This morning, after boiling the herbs for ten minutes (the stench!), I strain the muddy liquid into a mug and hesitate. Take deep breaths. Hesitate longer. Finally, with a deep sigh, I chug it back. Try not to gag.

Like mule piss on the Grand Canyon's Bright Angel Trail. At noon. In August.

The tea, as my acupuncturist likes to miscall it, does take the pain down a notch so I can function. It doesn't last, is not a cure, but helps me get through the day.

15

Searching for Miracles

Janet

Every time Janet and Steve face a new setback, they ask themselves: What do we need to do? The most frightening questions, though, are the ones they hardly dare to voice: Will what we do make any difference at all? Is there really anything we can do?

Without a magical crystal ball, outcomes can only be presumed, based on research, doctors' experience, and the path chosen.

Deciding what to do next raises even larger questions, ones that loom.

When does the continual search for treatment become folly? Does acceptance become resignation? Does facing reality mean giving up, or giving in to one's fate—whatever that means. Whose voice do we listen to?

When Janet and Steve return home to Annapolis from San Antonio, Steve pores over medical journals, talks to oncologists, and continues developing his own protocol for Janet's treatment. But answers elude him and every step feels like an eternity—time they don't have. For the first time in his life, he is beset with blinding migraines.

Janet prays for a miracle.

Miracles. People believe in them or they don't. Definitions vary. Some consider miracles strictly a biblical thing: Jesus walking on water, Moses parting the Red Sea; or more specifically, a Catholic thing: visions of Mary appearing, saints' bodies not decomposing, statues weeping. Some find them in the everyday: young ospreys knowing they should head south in the autumn after their parents have left them behind, a driver surviving a terrible crash, twins finding each other decades after separation at birth. Or find them in sports, like the acclaimed 1980 Olympic Miracle on Ice, when the ragtag amateur U.S. hockey team beat the Russian powerhouse in Lake Placid.

Steve is no proponent of miracles, of spontaneous healings. He believes more in prayer and positive thinking than in lightning bolts from heaven. When a calamity occurs, you set a path that makes sense, you pray you are on the right path, and you run as far and as fast as you can. When you are about to collapse, you hand the baton and hope God grabs it. You have to be willing to do the hard work first.

But this time, with the failure of the radiation to eradicate the tumors, both Steve and Janet know they are in trouble. Even Steve doesn't rule out looking for a miracle. Janet leads the search; she's done it before.

Nine years ago, three months before Janet would be diagnosed with cancer, Stephanie was born with a rare heart disease, Tetralogy of Fallot. She had open-heart surgery when she was four days old. Dread, like a snarling animal, lived in Janet's gut during those first days, especially during Steph's surgery. She sat with Steve and Lynn, saying Novenas. The surgeon had offered narrow hope. Stephanie had a 20 percent chance of surviving the surgery, a 10 percent chance of surviving to her first birthday. If she did survive, she would need subsequent open-chest, open-heart surgeries at ages one, three, and twelve plus multiple catheterizations.

Steph survived and she spent the following five weeks at Children's National Medical Center. Every morning, Janet pulled a sleepy Reid from his bed, strapped him into his car seat by 6 a.m. then drove to the hospital, a forty-five-minute commute barring bad traffic. She'd hand Steve a change of clothes; he'd spent the night there on a pullout bed. Then he'd shower, dress, and drive to his IRS job on North Capitol Street.

After work, Steve returned to the hospital for two hours with his family before Janet and Reid went home. Continual time with Steph was critical.

"The window on controlling pain with kids is narrow," Stephanie's doctor had explained to them. "The child hurts too much on the one side, but coma and death wait on the other. So we tend to let kids cry. But without reassurance and contact, they can eventually become desensitized and so distant they are difficult to reach. Everything hurts, so they shut everything off." Janet and Steve tried to make sure someone was always holding her.

When Janet arrived at 7 a.m., she'd find Steve rocking Steph, sometimes feeding her, sometimes thumping her back to prevent pneumonia. All those tubes and wires in such a tiny body. It took her breath every time she walked in. After Steve readied for work, kissed them all and left, Janet got out toys for Reid, and they settled in for the day.

What a luxury when they could take their baby home. But one afternoon, when Steve returned from work and bent over to cuddle Steph, she cried hysterically. Boggled, Steve and Janet shook their heads.

"Why is she crying like that?" Steve said. "It's like she looked at me and panicked."

"I know. It's weird. She wasn't upset until you walked in," Janet said, holding Steph close. "Oh! Steve, look at your shirt. It's white. I wonder if she thinks it's a doctor's coat and you're a doctor."

Laughing, Steve changed his shirt, pulling on a red T-shirt. Steph accepted his open arms and snuggled in. After that, Steve made sure he wore only colored shirts.

Steph's survival was a miracle in itself, but a year later, after her own surgery to remove half her palate, Janet went looking for another. In the spring of 1990, a month after Steph underwent her second open-heart surgery, she sought divine help from Ralph DiOrio, a priest in Sturbridge, Massachusetts known for his healing ministry. Steve, Janet, their mothers, and Steph went to his church, a ballroom-sized room holding two thousand people.

The priest held Steph over the altar and said she was cured. Janet couldn't stop smiling. She knew her baby would be fine.

Now, seven years later, with the failure of the San Antonio radiation, once again Janet is ready to search for a miracle. This time for herself.

16

Garabandal

Janet

April 1997

Staring out the glass of the Madrid airport on a quiet April afternoon, Janet wonders what's out there beyond the tarmac, behind the rise of brown hills. She sighs. Her weariness is palpable. They are waiting for a small plane to arrive, but it's socked in fog somewhere. Janet visualizes it as a small animal sleeping under a gray blanket, a small animal that needs to wake up. "Hurry," she whispers to it. She needs a miracle and will not be deterred. She is going to Garabandal.

Janet learned about Garabandal from her mother. Doris typed for a blind man, Joey Lomangino, of faith so strong he led annual pilgrimages to the village where, in the early 1960s, four young girls had seen visions of the Virgin Mary and the archangel Michael.

The shock of speaking with the Virgin transported the girls into religious ecstasy. They listened with eyes wide and heads thrown back to Mary's messages. Expectant visitors flocked to the tiny mountain village. Anonymously, pilgrims placed tokens— rings, rosaries, and crucifixes—on a table for the girls to collect and hold up to the Virgin to kiss. Afterwards, the girls walked through the crowds, their young faces shining with peace, handing the objects to their rightful owners, who they had never met. People claimed that as years passed, the kissed objects retained a certain odor and glow.

After four years and over two thousand apparitions, the visions stopped. By 1965, the girls no longer saw Mary or angels. The Vatican withheld an official opinion on the events, but pilgrimages continued to the spot where many felt miracles had happened and might happen again.

After Janet's despondent return from San Antonio in January, Doris found space for four on Lomangino's Easter expedition. The trip was long and travel complicated for Janet, but she jumped at the chance. Doris, Steve, and Lynn made up the party. Janet's self-consciousness about her scarred face was only part of her difficulty. More critically, her ravaged mouth still bled from the radiation, and she needed privacy when struggling to eat. Swallowing had become more difficult; she would gag, and food would spill from her mouth or come out her nose. Doctors had offered a feeding tube, a temporary one for vital nutrition, but Janet wouldn't hear of it. How can I feel like a whole person with that thing sticking out of me?

With the failure of the San Antonio radiation, Janet knew the tumor was growing. She needed hope. Nothing was going to stop her from seeking a miracle.

Fate tried.

Steve and Janet were to drive to Doris's house in New York before the flight. Loading luggage that morning, Steve discovered a puddle of gas underneath the car. Ever resourceful, he found a spare fuel line in his garage and fixed the leak. At Doris's house on Long Island, they called for an airport shuttle.

It never showed.

So they piled into Lynn's car and drove to the airport. Steve and Lynn dropped Doris and Janet at the curbside check-in with the luggage, then headed off to park.

The parking shuttle never came.

Shaking their heads and swearing, Steve and Lynn jogged three miles to the airport and found a very relieved Janet. They made the flight to Madrid.

Now, waiting for the small plane for the leg of the journey to Santander near Garabandal, sitting amongst people she doesn't know as they lounge and sleep in the gate area, Janet tries to sneak a bite of food. She opens a yogurt container and dips her head, hopes no one will notice her spills, hopes she won't choke. She spoons a tiny amount to her lips and licks it off. When she finishes, she heads to the women's bathroom, picks the sink farthest from the door, and discreetly slips the obturator from her mouth.

I hate doing this in public, she thinks as she runs water over the bumpy molded pink surfaces. If anyone sees it, she hopes they'll think it's a retainer, like kids wear after braces. It's just so embarrassing. As she wrestles the obturator back into her mouth, she pictures her mother and repeats the mantra that strengthens her resolve: I want to be as good a mother for my children as you were—and still are—for me, Mom. I won't quit. I can't.

Janet returns to the hard plastic chair and leans into Steve. She pictures the small plane nestled in gloom, and wills the fog, and the plane, to lift. Images of rising fog float her back in time to early mornings at The Digger when low mist hung over the water, bright sun threatening to dispel the mystery and magic.

The Digger. The very name makes her smile. Nobody knows why it was called The Digger, but oh, how she and her sisters loved to explore the gorge's banks. Summer days found them tramping across the road to scurry into the deep depression by the railroad tracks, their imaginations fueling their games. Poking around, they filled empty peanut butter jars with water and plopped in pollywogs to wait for legs; stuffed their pockets with blueberries to eat with milk and sugar. On lucky days, they got to ride in Little Grandpa's motorboat, either trolling The Digger or fishing Great South Bay. The sisters nicknamed him Little Grandpa because he lived in a one-story house.

Remembering, Janet feels ease flow through her. Her sister has relaxed as well as she can, curling across two seats, her mouth open, her breathing heavy. "What a bunch of Bohunks," Czechoslovakian Little Grandpa had called Lynn, Donna, and the cousins, his brown-haired tribe in the backyard plucking chickens. Small-boned and strawberry-blond, Janet was different. His China Doll.

But she liked to feel tough. As a fifth-grader at St. Mary's School, she persuaded Father McGovern to let her drum with the boys in the new Fife and Drum Band, not play the fife with the girls. Her talent bettered most of the boys. She drummed throughout her school years, her sisters playing fifes. Then after high school, they joined the Bayport Fire Department Fife and Drum. She recalls the championships she won. All those trophies!

The public address system crackles an announcement that sends applause rippling through the gate area where people and luggage crowd the chairs and floor. After seven hours of wondering when and if they would ever leave, they learn the plane will arrive shortly. Janet shakes her sister. "Lynn, wake up! The plane's almost here. We're going!"

Following the brief flight, their bus slowly ascends the thirty-five miles of narrow, twisting mountain roads. Her fatigue, self-consciousness, and despair fade as Janet thrills at the views of distant blue peaks, her stomach jumping when they descend toward the remote village of Garabandal.

As their bus pulls into the town nestled amongst the rolling hills and jagged crests of the Cantabrian Mountains, Janet delights in the velvety brown cows walking down the street. And the houses. "Oh, Lynn, look. Now I really feel like I'm back in Europe." A recollection of youth spreads through her, spirited back to the days of her early twenties when she traveled around Europe with ease.

The houses are stonework, apart from their wooden doors, and the village has the feel of permanence, of durability. Winter is relinquishing its hold, but as they descend the bus steps, chilly air swirls around them.

"I feel like we've gone back in time," Janet whispers to Steve.

Their lodging with an American expat couple now living in Garabandal offers the modern novelty of running water. The other twenty pilgrims are housed by townsfolk who live on second floors, above the warmth rising from the stalls of cows and sheep.

In 1961, when the apparitions began, Garabandal was an isolated community of eighty homes. Three hundred people lived there with their chickens and cows, sheep and goats. They farmed the rocky soil and withstood ferocious mountain winters as their ancestors had for centuries. At sunset, a bell called these devout Catholics to prayer in the Church of San Sebastian. Into the 650-year-old stone church, under the vaulted ceilings, amidst stone statues of Mary, Jesus, and the village patron San Sebastian, the townspeople gathered to say the rosary and litanies to the Virgin Mary. Little has changed.

Like the villagers, these travelers have their own routine of daily tours to shrines and sacred spots. They, too, are creatures of faith, each carrying hopes that this place of miracles will offer the grace they seek.

On one tour, the lunch is sandwiches on hard crusty rolls. Janet cannot eat them; her mouth barely opens and is still sore from radiation. No utensils were included to cut up the chunks of meat and cheese.

Stomach growling, she trudges up the hillside toward the cathedral with the others, trying not to feel sorry for herself. Then Steve whoops.

"Janet! Look!"

Sticking out of a bush is a fork.

As Janet climbs the steep footpath to her favorite spot for the last time, she stops to catch her breath and tighten her blue scarf to corral her profusion of hair, wild and brittle after the radiation. She folds her arms around herself, snugging her puffy turquoise jacket close against the cool air. The sun has set behind the mountains, giving the sky a pink glow. Through the stillness, she hears the clang of cowbell and the distant chatter of choughs—a flock of black birds wheeling toward the cliffs. It's Good Friday, their last night in Garabandal.

"Janet," Lynn calls. "Steve and I are waiting. It was your idea to take one more trip to the Pines, remember? Hurry up!"

"Yeah, yeah, I'm coming."

The rocky trail turns to dirt, hard-packed from expectant footfalls. New shoots of grass green the landscape. Snow lingers on the mountaintops.

One more trip to the Pines, she thinks, echoing Lynn's words with each determined step. Back to the place where miracles happen. I have to get up there again.

Of all the places they've visited over the course of the week, it's the Pines, Los Pinos, where the girls saw the visions of Mary, that have eased Janet's spirit most.

With Steve and Lynn, she treks to the first of fourteen stations of the cross. Janet gazes at the painting of Jesus. Though she's heard this story for forty years, she never tires of it.

"I know why you took your friends to the Garden of Gethsemane," Janet whispers. "You couldn't face what you knew was coming alone. I know that feeling. I don't know what I would do without Steve and Lynn, Mom, Donna, and my whole family."

At each station, where large depictions of Jesus's last days are tucked into moss-covered stones and caressed by vines, Janet prays, talking to Jesus like a companion. She has always prayed to Jesus, to Mary, to saints, to God, but here, in the Pines, Janet can feel their presence. She has never been anywhere like this, where every step feels sacred, where self and spirituality commingle like oxygen and blood.

At the fifth station, she sees Simon of Cyrene carrying the cross for Jesus. His generosity, in the face of hatred and disdain, touches her. "I'll help too," she whispers.

She prays for Steph and Reid, for Rita—a woman she has met on the trip whose daughter committed suicide—for her mom, for Steve, for her siblings, for everyone she can think of, including herself. Deep in meditation, she asks for a sign. "Please, let me know You are listening..."

Whoooosssshhh! A sudden wind blasts through the tops of the pines. Thick grey clouds roil, grasses flatten, leaves on low shrubs spin in disarray.

Lynn grabs Janet's arm. "Let's get out of here!" she yells above the roar. Lynn runs down the hill, but the wind catches her and blows her over onto her butt.

Janet laughs. She laughs and laughs and laughs. She can't help herself. "Sorry, Lynn, but that was so funny."

Lynn gets up, unscathed, and brushes off the dirt. The first gusty shriek has moved on, but a strong wind continues to blow, the sky growing gloomier.

"Let's head back," Lynn says, grabbing Janet's arm again.

"No," Janet says. "I want to finish the stations."

"It is going to get dark soon," Steve counters.

"No. I'm staying here."

Together, they climb the steep winding path, the wind rustling their jackets. Lynn giggles. "I know this place is really spiritual," she says, "but that was scary, almost supernatural...but I guess, not really... more like a religious sound swooshing through the pines. I mean, you believe in God so much, but you don't expect Him to actually show up!"

Tomorrow, they head home. When they reach the pines, Janet scours the branches looking for a pinecone. Not finding any, she realizes how much she yearns for one. Then, there it is. One, and only one. But it's too high for her to reach.

"Steve, will you please pick that cone for me?" she asks, pointing up at it. "I'd like to take one home."

"No, Janet. I don't steal."

"It's not stealing. And I only want one. Please."

"No. It's like taking something sacred."

"Oh, c'mon Steve. Pretty please. I really, really want one. Please." Janet knows she is groveling, but she can't help it. She longs for a memento of this place, of this soul-awakening experience. As she slumps onto a rock under the trees, waves of anger and frustration turn her recent laughter into tears. What a mess I am, she thinks.

Then she looks down. All around her are tiny pinecones, barely half-inch long. Kneeling, she collects a dozen, then a few more, tucks them into an empty film canister. She sits back on her heels and breathes a prayer of gratitude.

First, the fork, and now these pinecones. Tiny miracles. Maybe there is hope after all.

17

AG3340—The Prinomastat Years

Janet

APRIL 1997–2004

Kids and dogs greet Steve and Janet when they return from Garabandal, from days of spiritual surrender and prayer. Hugs, supper, showers. Their own bed. How relaxing to be home. But Steve knows he has work to do. Their souls feel refreshed, but deep fear still shrouds any new sense of promise.

Steve's research leads him to propose two questions: If tumors use molecular pathways to entice the body to generate blood vessels to keep them alive, how do we inhibit as many of these pathways as possible. Second, how do we keep tumors from shutting off the apoptosis process, which programs cancer cells to periodically die and be replaced. His early writing on these questions create interest in the oncology community and later will develop into his own thesis on treatment for Janet.

Right now, he studies MMP inhibitors. MMPs, or matrix metalloproteinases, are enzymes typically inactive in the body. If they become active, they can spur the metastasis of cancer. During a recent exam, Janet tested positive for three different MMPs. Steve knows they need to stop these enzymes.

"One MMP inhibitor is called AG3340," he explains to Janet. Playing below their second-floor screened porch are Steph, Reid, and Reid's new pet baby mallard, a Confirmation present from a neighbor. "My contacts at the National Cancer Institute say it looks promising, and I just found out this morning that the Food and Drug Administration has approved the drug for trial. I called the principal investigator at North Shore University Hospital in New York."

"You called him?" Janet says. "What did you say? What did he say?"

"'I want to get my wife in your trial,' I said.

"'What trial?' he asked.

"'Your AG3340 trial.'

"'It's not approved yet,' he says.

"'Yes, it is. Would you like to know your FDA number?'

"'Uh, hello? What are you talking about?'

"'I have it here. You've been approved.'

"'Really?'

"'I'm not lying to you. Can my wife get into your trial?'

"'There is no trial.'

"'Yes, there is. Does this make her first?'

"'Well, yeah, I guess it does.'"

"Steve," Janet laughs, "you crack me up. How do you keep doing this?"

As Steve goes over details and upcoming appointments, Janet feels a familiar mixture of pride and guilt. "Steve," she says, placing her hand on his, "I can't believe what you go through for me."

Steph and Reid and the duckling splash in the kiddie pool, a grateful respite from the whirlwind of all-things-medical.

"Time for bed," Janet calls. Reid scoops up the little duck he's named Chuck, a name that will remain even when Chuck turns out to be a girl duck, and he and Steph troop up the back steps. Reid plops Chuck into Janet's lap, and immediately Dan and Woody crowd around to snuffle the little feather bundle, Woody especially jealous of this intrusion. Chuck flutter-climbs up Janet's blouse until she reaches the top of her head. Poking and fussing with Janet's hair, the duckling nestles down, closes her eyes, and falls asleep.

AG3340, later called Prinomastat, is tested on one thousand people with macular degeneration or cancer. Janet is one of thirty in the trial for hard tumors, the only one with adenoid cystic carcinoma.

The trial begins with three rounds of Taxol chemotherapy treatment. Steve and Janet know the chemo won't work, but it's required for the AG3340. Between her second and third treatments, Janet's hair falls out. Eight-year-old Steph is upset, but when her mom's hair grows back, soft as velour, she loves stroking it like she does her Beanie Babies stuffed animals.

As the family settles into their home routines, Janet learns this new drug carries ugly side effects.

Starting AG3340 at 100 mg a day, she develops arthralgia, an arthritic pain so severe it's agonizing to push the button of the car handle to open it, to turn the key in the ignition. Skin peels off her hands as though burned.

The doctors are experimenting with a new dosing regimen: Give the patient as much as she can tolerate, then when the side effects become disabling, ratchet it down by a power of ten. The traditional regimen starts at a lower dose and slowly increases. But they are not sure how inhibitors will be tolerated.

After three months at 100 mg, Janet stops taking AG3340 for thirty days to clear any remnants of the inhibitor out of her system. She feels better, but the tumor is growing. The doctors put her back on 10 mg a day.

Janet's disabling pain returns.

So does Steve's.

Blinding headaches reappear as his own despair sets in. With every setback, with every new devastation, Steve's complex migraines pull his vision into a dot. Each time, he must sit in a quiet space and breathe meditatively for twenty minutes. Then the headache dissolves, his vision opens, and he can see again. Until the next one.

Striving for answers about the best dosage for the AG3340, Steve contacts a Vanderbilt University professor of cancer research who has helped him navigate treatments. This professor, one of the principal investigators on the AG3340 trial, introduces Steve to another PI who can better answer his dosage question.

"What's going on? Why is the trial bombing out?" Steve asks. "She started at 100 mg, can't handle ten, and now they want to put her on one."

"I probably shouldn't be telling you this," the investigator says, "but 1 mg won't work."

"What do you mean?"

"We've done a little preclinical work here and it looks like the minimal dosage is around two. She might even be better off taking 3 mg—one in morning, midday, and at night."

That's what Steve asks for when he calls the research doctor who has been prescribing the drug for Janet.

"Who are you to be messing around in my trial?" he says.

Steve slams down the phone receiver. He paces the kitchen, his mind seething until a realization strikes: This doctor thinks he's in charge, but he's not in charge of anything.

Steve's recourse is higher up, to the drug company. "I have preliminary information that your trial is flawed. Your drug might work, but not in the dosages you are trying."

But one determined husband, no matter how well informed, cannot change a clinical trial. For months Steve tries. Finally, he contacts the director of the Compassionate Release Program for the Food and Drug Administration. Under this program, a drug company can release a questionable drug out of the goodness of its heart to an individual who has exhausted all other treatment options.

"What are you trying to do?" the director asks Steve.

"I am trying to change the trial protocol."

"Why don't you just do that?"

"I have been trying for four months."

"Well, all they have to do is request it and we'll say yes."

"Really?"

Steve calls the drug company back.

"You need to change your protocol," he tells them.

"We can't change it."

"Want to bet. I know who can."

Not knowing how to respond, the drug company tries to shuttle Steve off to lawyers. But Steve doesn't want to talk to lawyers. He wants to talk to doctors and PIs.

Eventually he writes a letter outlining the problem, its solution, and the drug company's idiocy for not listening to reason. He sends a copy to the drug company and threatens to send it to the New York Times, the National Cancer Institute, and the FDA.

Finally, the trial is changed.

Janet begins taking 2.5 mg pills twice a day, which she tolerates well. She continues to take AG3340, later called Prinomastat, for seven years even though the drug company abandons it after six because it does not seem to work. A thousand people entered the trial, thirty in Janet's hard tumor trial. Of those thousand, Prinomastat worked for only two.

One of those two is Janet.

18

Driving
the Gorge

Dotty

JANUARY 1998

At least it's not snow or ice, I think, as I pass a triple trailer in a January downpour, cringing as a blast of spray shoots over my station wagon, leaving me for countless seconds in a gray nightmare. I forge ahead and return to the right lane, letting out first a sigh of relief, then one of exasperation as I drive back to White Salmon on the Oregon side of the Columbia River from yet another doctor's appointment in Portland. The GI doctor I saw, whose looks reminded me of sixteen-year-old Neil Patrick Harris from the old TV show Doogie Howser, M.D., pissed me off. I've spent the last twenty minutes ranting to the steep walls rising in the mist.

"You didn't even listen," I say aloud. "You may look like Doogie, but you certainly are no Doogie. Doogie would have found an answer. You couldn't see past your own ego."

That morning, after an examination and tests, the young doctor called me into his office. "Menstrual cramps," he declared as the cause of my gut pain. "And I am going to have you see a rheumatologist for your back." Are you insane? I'd wanted to scream. Cramps! Is that what you tell all your female patients? Cramps—even if the pain lasts all month? And rheumatism? Please. How did they ever let you out of medical school? I wish I'd had the nerve to say something to him directly. Instead, I walked out, fuming inside.

Hands on the wheel, I pull again into the left lane to pass a slow green Toyota. I need to return in time to meet Ruth and her fourth-grade friends after school for the Junior Girl Scout meeting. I am the leader of Ruth's troop, plus an assistant for Helen's Brownie troop. I go over the list of materials I need to bring— sewing machine, fabric, thread, scissors, patterns.

Learning that some children at the local Headstart did not have warm clothes, the girls decided to make fleece mittens and scarves for them. They have already designed and created a special box for the clothes. If a child comes to school without mittens or needs a warm scarf, they borrow them from the box, even take them home. My Girl Scouts, like I, want to make a difference in other people's lives.

The cold dreary winter also has the girls looking ahead to spring, making plans to go on a hike at Catherine Creek on the Washington side of the river toward The Dalles. The wildflowers there put on a spectacular show, and I hope I'll find the usual joy I feel from the washes of yellow-gold balsamroot studded with blue lupine, from the charm of the tiny purple grass widows. But wildflowers feel far away.

Pain scorches my abdomen, the pain that never leaves me now. Desperation clings like hot wax. Two weeks ago, I surreptitiously cut off a hank of my hair, in the back near my scalp where it wouldn't show, and sent it along with $100 we couldn't afford to a woman who claimed she could figure out what was wrong with me. When her diagnosis came, I barely glanced at it; there was nothing of use. I ripped it up and threw it away. How embarrassing to have reached this level of hopelessness, trying anything to stop hurting. I never keep secrets from Jonathan. I tell him everything. But I could not admit this.

The rain pours without letup. Oncoming traffic speeds past me headed west towards the city. I nod as tears leak from the corners of my eyes. Though a barrier prevents it, I feel how easy it would be to turn the wheel to the left and aim straight for those approaching headlights. I will not, I cannot, but at this moment, I understand those who do.

19

The Move to Annapolis

Dotty

JUNE–SEPTEMBER 1999

In bathing suits, shorts, and water shoes, we trek the slick wooden steps into Oneonta Gorge, leaving the 95-degree heat of June up on the highway. We've left towels and dry clothes in the car for our wet return.

Timid at first to put our feet in the frigid water, we hop from one smoothed stone to another until the inevitable wide gap when we are forced to wade, shouting with shock and delight.

I watch a gray American dipper as he nimbly flies from rock to rock, now dunks his head into the water looking for a nibble of lunch. Oh, how I adore seeing these birds, equally for their finesse in the tumbling waters of rivers and streams, and because it means I, too, am there. As though to seal the deal, the sweet cascade of canyon wren notes echoes from somewhere up on the 150-foot cliffs, and his resultant buzz at the end makes me laugh out loud. Oh happy day!

Ruth, Helen, and her friend Robin scramble over the boulders with a boost from Jonathan and me; we gasp as we slide into water up to knees and thighs. Giggling all around, we swish forward in the lush cool greenness—the basalt canyon walls awash with many species of ferns, including maidenhair fern with its perfect open-fan shape, plus lichens and mosses.

When we reach the final stretch, it's decision time. We can see the snowmelt torrent of Lower Oneonta Falls ahead, but to reach its splash and emerald wonderland cove, we must either wade in deep icy water through a narrow canyon or walk a precipitous series of ledges along the cliff face. Sometimes in the past, we have chosen to just stop here. But this is our last chance.

Glancing at each other, we nod and charge ahead through the cold, howling and trying to catch our breath. Jonathan and I hold the girls' hands to steady them on the stony bottom, and push forward to the pool, where the water is only slightly less deep. We revel in the thunderous thrill of the falls. We don't want to leave, but the girls and I are shivering. We hug each other, grin, and begin the slippery walk back.

I stand at the sink and look out at rufous humming-birds searching for their missing nectar feeder in the redbud tree we planted, and at the blooming rose bushes we inherited when we moved here seven years ago when Jonathan left his job with the National Park Service in Philadelphia to be the director of the Columbia River Gorge Commission.

Our one-story house had a small kitchen, so Jonathan designed and built this new one with the help of a local contractor. The wide picture window offers prime views of our garden and the humming-birds; of the varied thrush that tucks under our giant spruce in winter; of Daisy the dachshund who prances up Pucker Huddle Road each morning patrolling the neighborhood; of Old Yeller, the large yellow cat that has adopted us and our neighbors, relying on them for food, on us for a dish of milk which we use to entice him out of the rafters of our garage each night. Now, we're packed up. It's time to move again.

Seven years and no one has been able to find an answer for my gut pain. Doctors have poked, prodded, and shook their heads. I've endured barium x-rays, laparoscopic explorations, acupuncturist needles. I got some relief from the Chinese herbs, but only the oxycodone I recently succumbed to taking every third night to try to get some sleep truly stops the pain. Until it wears off.

I did wonder about diet a couple of years ago after I churned homemade ice cream with Helen's Brownie troop and, after eating it, found my stomach too painful to touch. I stopped eating dairy and later found additional gut relief when I stopped eating corn, cucumbers, and bananas. And I, a confirmed addict, even gave up chocolate when I linked it to my migraines. But the intestinal pain has roared on. It'll take a waterfall to put out this fire.

Surveying the boxes stacked around the house, looking to see what I have missed, I realize it's time to try to pry Helen away from Robin. It won't be easy. We will miss so many close friends when we move—neighbors, teachers, families with children that have grown with ours. After quitting coaching three years ago, but still craving to be around kids, I turned to volunteering. For our Quaker meeting in The Dalles: taught First Day School and Quakerism 101, plus helped lead weekend retreats. For Ruth and Helen's elementary school: listened to new readers in kindergarten and first grade; offered a gifted-and-talented science program for fourth graders; sewed doll clothes for fundraisers. For the Junior Girl Scout troop: taught a wide range of crafts, took them hiking and camping, and co-ran summer day camps. I've just kept going.

Jonathan flies in tonight; the moving truck comes tomorrow. Then we'll depart for the East Coast, to Annapolis where Jonathan has already begun serving as the National Park Service director for the Chesapeake Bay Gateways Network, back to Maryland where my teaching career began. I head out the sliding glass door to our backyard and look south to Mt. Hood, to the Columbia River where windsurfers jump and glide like many-colored butterflies. Our once productive 1200-square-foot garden lies fallow. We didn't plant tomatoes, corn, or potatoes this year, though our basil, oregano, thyme, and rosemary plants are flourishing.

Every morning for the last two weeks, while Jonathan has been at his new job in Annapolis and Ruth at camp in Vermont, Helen and I have picked marionberries, red raspberries, and golden raspberries from our three long rows of head-high trellised vines, then I have cooked and canned jams of each kind. Jonathan is in mourning for these bushes, for the six pints of berries he picked each summer evening, mountains of berries finding their way onto his breakfast granola, into his pies and renowned fruit tarts. I hope the jams will help.

As I cut across the lawn toward the road, the wind pushes against me, the hot wind that has met me every summer day as I gardened while the girls played with friends in the sandbox or on the swing set we built; the blowing wind that dried my clothes on the line and one day came with a roar that scared me into the house only to see a swarm of bees the size of a cow tear through the yard. Sometimes, the blasting wind felt like too much, like one more thing I had to bear. On those days, I wanted to hide where it was quiet, where I didn't have to pretend vigor, where no one made demands of me, not even the wind.

Today, in mid-July, we drive across the country, celebrating Helen's ninth birthday in Idaho along the Snake River. As we pass ranches, Jonathan moos at every cow; on the open plains, we guess the distances to horizons; during late nights, Helen's stuffed animals take on their own personalities as I sing endless boisterous songs to keep us going. When we arrive in Annapolis, before we go to the house we've bought next to a 350-acre wooded park, we stop at the library and each get a library card. First things first.

It's hot, muggy—reminiscent of Upper Darby summers. My New England blood craves more moderate July temperatures. The dry wind of the gorge would be welcome right now as sweat pours from me as soon as I step out of the car. Indoors, I am grateful for central air conditioning, a first-time luxury for us. The moving van arrives and we have the movers stack the boxes in the middle of each room so we can paint every wall—yellows, spring green, cornflower blue—bringing the colors we love to our new home.

I buy a kayak, the first boat I have ever owned despite living next to water for most of my life. It becomes my tether, connecting me to the Bay.

To help ease all our transitions, we begin regularly attending Annapolis Friends Meeting, and after school begins, I start up Girl Scout troops: a Junior troop for girls Helen's age, a Cadette troop for Ruth's. Soon, a wonderful blend of girls from different schools and backgrounds meet weekly.

On this sunny late September afternoon, Ruth and the Cadette girls bustle around our kitchen setting out their snack and chatting about a service project painting a fence and planting seagrasses at the nearby Annapolis Maritime Museum. I sit on the living room couch reading over the health forms they've just handed in. All seem complete with the necessary information, but one stops me. I read it, then read it again. The health form belongs to fifth-grade Stephanie. There's a note from her mom, Janet, with a startling request: If Stephanie seems tired, please let her rest. She recently had heart surgery. I watch Steph pouring juice for the troop, chatting along with the rest of the middle-school-age girls. Okay, Janet, I think. I'll keep an eye out, but Steph looks like she's doing great. She certainly seems fine to me.

The next day, I meet Dr. Czapp, my new primary care physician. I describe my gut and back pain and explain how last night's supper of spaghetti intensified the burning. "Why don't you try giving up gluten," she says.

Ten years from now, gluten will become the hot topic of digestive malady, but it hasn't been getting any press in the '90s and isn't on many physicians' radars. One doctor of Eastern Medicine in Oregon had added gluten to my long list of what not to eat, but I had ignored it, thinking bread couldn't be causing this much pain.

Giving up gluten proves to be the kicker. Within a week, I feel better, seemingly miraculously, for days on end. In fact, I feel great, something I haven't been able to say in almost a decade. After some testing, I even have a diagnosis. Not the one I fear, celiac disease—for which every speck of gluten must be avoided—but irritable bowel syndrome. The coal fire in my gut is gone.

20

Back
to Normal

Dotty

FEBRUARY 2001

On a February afternoon, I arrive home to find Helen at the kitchen counter doing homework while Ruth bakes chocolate chip cookies for our trip to Ottawa, Canada to skate on the Rideau Canal. Low bright sun illuminates a spider web under a chair and sends rainbow swatches across the room as it gleams through window crystals. I collect a rainbow on the back of my hand and look at my daughters.

"Mom!" they chorus. "How did it go?" I try to find words, unsure how to begin.

After a year and a half here in Annapolis, I made the decision to go back to work. With my vitality renewed and the girls both at the middle school in the fall, I looked into teaching again. On a whim, I called Sandy Spring Friends School, the Quaker school just north of Washington D.C., where my career began over twenty years before, to see if they needed an upper school science teacher. They did, I applied, and today, after several interviews and teaching a class, I was offered the job. This would be my first time back to full-time work since the girls were born. Earlier waves of excitement that coursed through me at the school now feel muddled.

"I got offered the job," I tell them. "I'd be teaching upper school Biology, General Science, and AP Environmental Science. What do you think? It's forty miles away so I won't be here when you get home from school." Like I've always been, I think. Like Mom always was for me and Patty.

Ruth, thirteen and brimming with self-confidence, whips toward me, flinging her waist-length blond braid, and says, "Mom! That's great!" Then with a few exasperated shakes of her head, she gives me a hard stare as she points a spoonful of cookie dough at me. "But, Mom. Seriously? You're worried about us? We'll be fine."

And I know they will be, but I still feel burdensome guilt nudging at the corners of my decision. Helen, now an effusive ten-year-old, crows from a high kitchen stool, "Mom! You love teaching. And your friends work there. You'll love it—you have to do it!"

Somewhat assuaged but not totally convinced, I talk to Jonathan that night. Married for almost two decades, we have intermeshed our lives; we make a good team.

"Honey, that's fantastic," he says, hugging me. "Congratulations." And then, in his next breath, "Do you feel up to this?"

He's watched me deal with ten years of pain and exhaustion. Even after giving up gluten, it took more tweaking of my diet to completely calm my gut. He knows how much I enjoy students and being in the classroom, but also my tendency to be consumed by schoolwork. I can sense a degree of hesitancy within his heartfelt support, but inside, clarity unfolds. I ignore his ambivalence and feel my doubts recede.

"Jonathan, I promise I'll have time for school and you and the kids. It's going to be great!"

Buoyed by uncontrollable enthusiasm, I gush with plans for teaching again, my laughter, now his, nourishing my giddiness. My future feels so right. I feel as though my whole body is singing.

21

Onset

Dotty

FEBRUARY 2002

Six months into my renewed teaching career, I lurch into my science classroom in the February dimness of a gray 7 a.m. morning, laden with a backpack full of notebooks. In one hour, comments must be input into the computer for each of my seventy students, a biology experiment set up, and corrected lab books sorted into piles. But the head cold that laid me out all weekend still dogs me. Stuffy and sluggish, I drink from my water bottle to stifle a cough, and head to the computer.

Opening a file, I notice crooked lines of light in the upper left quadrant of my vision. Seriously. A migraine? Not needed right now. The physics teacher wanders in and catches me uttering my frustration aloud. When I admit my concern—how to get everything done in an hour with a migraine coming on—he says he will enter the comments.

"But, you know, you only had to write reports on the students who weren't doing well," he says, "not on all your students. These are interim reports, not regular comments."

I spent all weekend crawling out of bed to write seventy comments instead of five interims? I want to cry but instead, bash around trying to find the equipment for the lab experiment.

"Go home," he says. "I'll finish up here and get teachers to sub for you. Go home."

Angrier at my body for letting me down than grateful for this reprieve, I thank him and tromp to my car. An hour to drive here, now do it all over again? Ugh. I fling my backpack onto the passenger seat and head to Annapolis.

The mid-morning house is quiet. Ruth and Helen won't get off the bus from middle school until three; Jonathan will bike home from work at supper time. We only have one car—a decision we made when we moved here—less gas emissions, better for air quality, better for the Bay. I vaguely wonder why the migraine hasn't kicked in; usually, the bright, jagged aura lasts for about thirty minutes, then after a five-minute pause, the pain begins. I crawl into bed, pull the covers over my head, and snort in disgust. What a way to start my forty-fifth birthday.

Two hours later, I wake up. Still no pain. Well, that's good but weird. And the lights in my vision are still there, even with my eyes closed. Even weirder.

"An ocular migraine," Dr. Czapp's associate says, handing me a sample of Imitrex. "Sometimes there's no pain, just the aura." I don't believe a word of it. How can it be a migraine with no pain? I wish Dr. Czapp were in town. "If your eyes don't improve," he continues, "call an ophthalmologist."

The Imitrex does nothing. So, the next afternoon, Friday, I get home from school and call an ophthalmologist. She says, "Wait until morning. If your eyes don't improve, go to the emergency room for a CT scan."

The room gets smaller, just me and the phone in my hand. "Okay," I whisper out loud. "Remain calm. It doesn't hurt, it could be nothing. Breathe. No need to panic." Listen to Helen's plans for her sixth-grade science fair project. Drive to pick up Ruth from indoor crew practice.

The next morning, after two hours in the ER waiting room, I'm greeted by a cheery nurse for the scan. An hour later I leave, with reassurance there's no brain tumor.

Back at work on Monday, I update my science department colleagues. The head of the department audibly sighs. "I was hoping it wasn't a tumor," he says. Really? How did he know? A brain tumor hadn't even crossed my mind until the nurse mentioned it. So naïve. What don't I know? What is this?

Finally, Dr. Czapp returns. She tells me it's most likely this or that. I hear but do not process her words. She tells me to schedule an MRI. Immediately.

The next morning at breakfast I convince Jonathan to go to work. "It's just a test," I tell him. "We probably won't know the results for a couple days. I'll go get it done, then come home."

Careful to dress with no metal in my clothes—no zippers, no belt—I go to the medical center for the MRI.

Glasses, watch, boots off. Recline on the hard, cold, white slab. Pillow tucked under knees; bracket clamped around head. Breathe as the slab slides into the white tunnel. No claustrophobia, thank goodness. Must be a nightmare for some people. Close eyes and lie motionless, like the stillness used while worshipping in silence at Quaker meeting. Come up with metaphors for the sounds: the angry bellows of two differently-toned air horns, the ratcheting clamor of a slow jackhammer, the insistent banging of a fist on a metal drum. Forty minutes later, slide out for dye injection in arm, slide in for second half. Again, listen to noise clunk: the deafening monotone strum of an electric guitar going on and on, more air horn blasts, the repetitive clanging of crazed steeple bells. Wonder what these sounds do, what they are discovering.

Finally, it's over. I put on my jacket and head to the door when a receptionist stops me. "Dr. Czapp wants to see you in her office." My stomach dives. What? Right now? When does a doctor spontaneously put aside her other patients to see you immediately? What does she already know?

The elevator carries my pounding heart and too-wobbly-for-the-stairs legs to the sixth floor. Why didn't I ask Jonathan to come with me? Later, I'll learn he did try to find me but biked to the wrong clinic—one we used to go to.

Upon entering the waiting room, I'm called back to her office. The trembling begins in my core, as though an inner hive of bees has burst. Fold arms around ribs, try not to shake visibly. Butt on edge of chair in exam room, back straight. Ready, but for what?

Dr. Czapp enters, pulls over her stool, and sits facing me. We know each other well—she's been my doctor for three years. I read her melancholy face and brace myself.

"The scan shows white spots on your brain," she says, "which means there are damaged nerves. I am 99 percent certain of my diagnosis. I'm so sorry, Dotty. You have multiple sclerosis."

I envision wheelchairs.

22

Ice

Dotty

FEBRUARY 2002

A week later, with temperatures in the low 40s, my optimism lures me to the cove. Yes, the ice is breaking up. Smiling, I pat my kayak, haul it off the car and into the water. Ahhh. Even though my bow must crack through a skim of ice to reach open water, it feels so good, so right to be paddling on this overcast Saturday morning. Perhaps it's because my birth falls on the cusp between Aquarius and Pisces, but once I'm on, in, or next to water, my soul relaxes, my whole self finding its place of grace.

Scanning with binoculars, ignoring the jagged lights in my vision, I check for ducks. Far-away dots of canvasback mix with smatterings of bufflehead and scaup, but nothing swims nearby. Silence envelops me. Even the colors are muted, charcoals and faded blues. Distant tundra swans burst into the somber southern sky, their whiteness mesmerizing me. As they head toward the horizon, they glow in sharp contrast to the cloudy sky and slate-gray water. I feel the pang of approaching spring—soon they will head back to Alaska to breed.

Along the edges of the harbor, small fist-sized chunks of ice drift by, miniature icebergs to nudge aside with my hull. A broad half-inch-thick coat of ice undulates with the waves, its fissures grating one upon the other. A low persistent hum, like thousands of mosquitoes, invades the air.

I maneuver alongside a thick milky opaque layer whose long deep cracks protest only slightly, but near the docks, a wide sheet of transparent ice buzzes insistently. Continual, squeaky, loud.

I came to the Bay to look for ducks. Instead, I listen to ice.

23

Revelations

Dotty

FEBRUARY 2002

After Dr. Czapp said multiple sclerosis, I found my car and drove to Jonathan's office. I didn't know what else to do. My body couldn't stop shaking, my jaw shivering as though ice had entered the marrow of my bones. Hollow legs carried me to his office, my heart racing.

He was on the phone, Noticing me in the doorway, he said into the receiver, "Look, something has come up. Can I call you back later? Thanks."

"What's wrong?" he asked, jumping from his computer chair.

"Come outside," I whispered, not trusting my voice.

"Honey, what is it?"

He held my hand as we walked down the hall. I didn't answer until we were outdoors.

"Jonathan, Dr. Czapp says I have multiple sclerosis."

We stood in the snowy parking lot next to the Severn River's frozen harbor between Eastport and Annapolis and held each other. We didn't have words for this.

Later, I found Jonathan curled on the floor of our bedroom, sobbing. I could only guess at his thoughts, wondering if they matched mine. What does this mean? What's next? Will we get to keep traveling, hiking, birding? Again, we held each other, trying not to imagine the worst. But as he wept, I gritted my teeth. This was not going to stop me.

That night, the internet engrossed me—research being my default reflex. Unlike the decade of unknown abdominal pain, this time the disease came with a name, with websites. I read it all. MS was causing my immune system to attack nerve cells in my brain. The protective fatty myelin sheath around my optic nerve, like the insulation around a wire, was being damaged, affecting my sight.

Relieved to learn that MS is rarely fatal, I felt a bit disheartened by other aspects: no cure, progressive, erratic. No knowledge from one day, one minute, to the next of what might happen. Nothing...or paralysis. Or pain. Apparent perfect health...or the loss of bladder control, the ability to swallow, to speak, to stand, to think.

Predictability was gone, but self-care was under my control. To help stop the attack, I heeded my new neurologist's recommendation and administered a three-day course of nightly at-home intravenous high-dose steroids (long sleeves hid the IV catheter's PICC line in my forearm from students), followed by a month's slow dosage decrease of prednisone pills.

Seeing at a distance and driving still worked—the lights were in the sky portion of my vision—but fine detail posed a challenge. I asked my students to type as much of their work as possible to make it easier to read. The classroom was manageable, but another responsibility weighed on me.

Its forfeit would be doubly hard for me. I'd have to give up two things I hold tight.

Previous spring Intersessions found me backpacking with students all over the southwest in places I love—Big Bend in Texas, Organ Pipe National Monument in Arizona, Canyonlands in Utah, and the Grand Canyon where I had worked as a naturalist in the Student Conservation Association's intern program one year after graduating from Earlham College.

Earlham College: where Jim Cope taught me ornithology; where my first college friend, Elaine, greeted me on the field hockey field; where Jonathan and I first met in the science library while we worked in adjacent cubicles on a take-home Quantitative Ecology final during our sophomore year; and where I (and a year later, Jonathan) spent a three-month term off-campus on Southwest Field Studies, learning natural history, experiential education techniques, land use management, and wilderness skills—backpacking, cooking, rock-climbing, rappelling—throughout national parks and monuments in Arizona and Texas.

These skills allowed me to become a backcountry

111

instructor, but the program taught me so much more. Living with the same small group of people on that off-campus program for three months illuminated deep-rooted aspects of myself.

Most of my childhood weekends and afternoons were spent exploring the woods behind my house in southeastern Massachusetts or walking Buzzards Bay beaches, but now I realized how profoundly the natural world touched my soul. Everything's name became important: the birds and reptiles and mammals, the cacti, flowers, and bedrock below them, and how they all interacted. I was becoming the naturalist who would work on the North Rim of the Grand Canyon four years later. The outdoors was as necessary as breath.

So it was my very breath I feared losing as my ability to lead my upcoming wilderness Intersession—and perhaps more—became questionable.

Plus, another challenge loomed: Once more, I'd have to step out of my armor. Worse, I'd have to admit to myself I was not invincible.

Southwest Field Studies had given me an early lesson in how much I hid inside myself, never divulging my feelings of discouragement or sadness because those emotions felt like weakness. To be the best person meant being positive, never admitting to having a problem, and solving everything on my own. I'd spent my life proving I was tough.

But being stuck inside myself made it hard for me to know how to reach out to someone else. One day, at the end of a long backpacking trek in Big Bend National Park, we all flopped into camp, exhausted. But the sun was setting, and we needed to eat. My friend Jody had started a stove and begun cooking. Spontaneously, I knelt to rub her shoulders. In turn, an instructor massaged mine. The simplicity of shared touch moved me profoundly. It opened a chink in my armor, in my New England stoicism.

Quakers believe there is "that of God" in each person. We use the term Light to reference that Spirit. Perhaps that chink would allow Light both to flow out of me and flow in from others. Though I've developed and maintained good friendships, I've never let those friends see inside. Only God saw that.

Could I learn that showing unhappiness, trepidation, and uncertainty was not a sign of fragility? Would it help me to develop deeper and truer relationships, both with myself and others? When the instructor rubbed my shoulders, I recognized its connection to my failings. Why had I not understood this before I was twenty years old? And what, now, was I supposed to do with this new understanding?

This paradigm shift started my journey of opening to my feelings. Without this realization, without this shift, I don't think I ever would have had the courage and self-confidence to become a teacher.

Now my vulnerability was rearing its head again. More ferociously than ever before.

My students and I were to leave in less than a month for a two-week backpacking trip to visit and work with the Havasupai tribe at the bottom of the Grand Canyon. But not knowing how the disease was going to progress and unwilling to take chances with students, I chose to stay in Maryland. How could I take students into the wilderness when I could not trust my own body? I could not. Making that decision took my breath away.

I could scarcely breathe.

24

Spring Voices

Dotty

APRIL 2002

April in Annapolis abounds with blossoms as cherries, magnolias, redbuds, and dogwoods perform a succession of pink. Lime-colored leaves sprout; orange and yellow migrant birds flitter among them. When tundra swans leave in mid-March, ospreys replace them on the Bay, hauling long branches to rebuild last year's nests. The woods fill with song and with it my yearly practice of sifting through the voices, compartmentalizing the myriad of cardinal, robin, blue jay, titmouse, and wren songs to one part of my brain, so I can listen for the migrants— the gnatcatchers, vireos, orioles, and warblers. The hermit thrush that has frequented our heated birdbath all winter is gone, headed north. I wait for the wood thrush, the bell of the forest, to arrive from Central America.

The steroids, which kept me on a jittery high, are tapering to an end. I marvel at how they've affected my body—wobbly legs, full-body weakness, dry mouth, clogged ears. I can't seem to drink enough water to stay hydrated, nor eat enough food to keep up with my metabolism. I've lost ten pounds in three weeks. My body learned what it feels like to be hungry—when hunger pangs go beyond "growling" to become gnawing pain. I sleep two to three hours a night, then lie awake, feeling my heart pound a hundred beats per minute. I make it through the week of the local Intersession, thankful I have not dared take my students west. During the second week of spring break, when I join my family and in-laws on the Outer Banks of North Carolina for Easter vacation, all I can do is sleep.

Exhaustion becomes my everyday life, long after the steroids have left my system. Not the tired you get from pulling an all-nighter. Not the tired you feel after putting in a full day of work. But absolute and utter fatigue.

No amount of sleep can banish the feeling of depletion. I wake as worn down as when I went to bed and fight to keep up with my schoolwork. I know what it's like to be awake all night with a crying baby and still need to function the next day, but this is different. My entire being is seeping away.

I need to listen to my body. A persistent voice, the voice of my spirit, keeps warning me, buzzing at me, insisting I need to change course. So—I do what I always do.

I ignore it.

25

Summer Stretch

Dotty

JUNE–JULY 2002

"Jonathan!" I call as he comes in the back door from work. "I won the summer scholarship! They give me a new laptop, and a two-week course at Bullis School learning to use it. Specifically for teaching my classes. Homework assignments, project descriptions, everything will be on my own website."

"That's wonderful," he says, congratulating me and giving me a big hug, but I can feel his skepticism.

"Jonathan. It'll be fine," I assure him. "I know, I know...I'll have to drive an hour and a half around the D.C. beltway during both rush hours. And the drive home is after being in class all day. I know you'll be in Poland for two of the three weeks. But I'll be fine. It's gonna be so cool."

The school semester ends, and I breathe the relief of no commitments—at least for a week. Then I take Ruth and Helen to summer camp in Vermont, which involves flying to Providence, Rhode Island, driving a rental car to Jonathan's family's house in New Hampshire where the girls pack up their trunks, then driving over to camp to drop them off. Afterwards, I drive down to visit Mom in Massachusetts, trying to hide my exhaustion as I make meals—some to eat, some to freeze—plus take her to appointments and weed her gardens.

Back home in Annapolis, I rest for two weeks before the computer class begins and make plans to conserve energy during the course. I set up carpooling with another Annapolis teacher and arrange to spend one night with friends who live near Bullis. I have complete confidence it will work.

"Look at this!" I hold up my new PC to Jonathan as he walks in after my first day. "I learned to write code today. And here's the opening page of my new website with a photo I took of the lake in New Hampshire as the backdrop."

I put up my feet while Jonathan cooks bacon, slices tomatoes from our garden, washes lettuce, toasts bread—his, plus my gluten-free variety. Not wanting to leave my perch when he announces the BLTs are ready, I reluctantly head to the kitchen to pour our water and light the candles as he brings our open-face sandwiches. We hold hands across the table as we've done since we met at Earlham, though there we held hands in a circle that included our ten housemates gathered every suppertime at our funky off-campus house. In Quaker-custom silence, I pray for those who need healing or extra Light in their lives and give thanks. So much for which to be grateful.

I am continually grateful for Jonathan. To make life easier for me, and because it nourishes his creative side, Jonathan does most of the cooking, as he has done since White Salmon days when pain consumed me. A fabulous and flexible chef, he has handled my dietary changes with ease. His culinary talents were revealed early in our Earlham relationship, baking me a sublime Black Forest cherry cake when I visited his Rochester, New York home. Ten years later, for my thirtieth birthday, while we were leading Southwest Field Studies—the same program we had gone on as students—he made me another of those elaborate cakes, this time at a campground on the Rio Grande in a tin oven over a Coleman stove.

After cleaning up tonight's supper, he reads the Washington Post, while I unlock the mysteries of building a Dreamweaver website. "This is so cool," I keep uttering. Every evening finds me studying on the couch, PC on lap, notebook open beside me on the long game table Jonathan made for me.

Feeling lonely when we moved to Annapolis and mourning the loss of our beautiful White Salmon backyard, Jonathan created the table. Burning in outlines, he then painted a red and purple chessboard on one end, and in the center, a cerulean, lavender, and peach scrabble board that flipped to a multicolored Chinese checkers board with a drawer underneath for pieces. At the other end, the Monopoly board properties are titled with beaches and mountains we love plus roads where we have lived: in Richmond, Indiana's Earlham off-campus houses (the light blue cheap properties), in Upper Darby, in White Salmon. Cribbage holes with accompanying skunks line the teal perimeter.

Between the game boards and cribbage, he outline-burned and painted a border of favorite memories from our lives together: Mt. Hood, our berry bushes, the gorge. Apponagansett meetinghouse in my hometown where we were married, our family house in New Hampshire, iconic foods like fluffernutters, the clambake I worked at since I was eleven. It holds our lives, and now, my overflow of work.

In the second week of the computer class, while scanning slides from desert backpacking trips to teach about plant adaptation, I feel it happen. An odd sensation, as though a hole has opened in the sole of my sneaker and everything inside me has poured out. I keep scanning. Put my left elbow on the narrow table, lay my head in my hand. But the dark pain of exhaustion grips my core. The afternoon looms long. Too long.

"I need to leave early today," I tell the instructor. He sighs. He does not answer but shakes his head. The implication that I am wasting his time and squandering this privileged opportunity is not lost on me. None of these instructors know about my MS, and it's impossible to explain how it feels. I look fine, the picture of health. Only I know I am no longer here.

And Jonathan so far away in Poland.

26

Blazing Stars

Dotty

SEPTEMBER 2002

Like iron drawn to a magnet, I paddle across Duvall Creek to a small cove on this quiet September morning. A thrill washes over me. The blazing stars are blooming. Even under clouded skies, these wildflowers' two-foot stalks gleam with dozens of tiny purple tubular flowers. With unabashed waves of color, they cover this small hillside—the only place I have ever seen them—marking it as their spot, their space, their home.

A year from now, these shores will be pummeled by the storm surge created by Hurricane Isabel. A nearby sycamore, its broad branches a favorite osprey perch, topples into the waves. Seven-foot seas on top of high tides inundate shorelines, small islands, and spits, leaving wayward docks and shards of wood in their wake. People whose homes look straight out to the Bay wake to eroded front yards and water coursing down hallways. Naval Academy classrooms flood, and kayakers paddle through the streets of downtown Annapolis.

Howling winds roar all night. At 1:50 a.m., some-thing crashes into the side of our house. Helen and I wake up. We creep downstairs, and open the front door to peer into the pelting rain, and find the gaping hole a huge fallen limb has made in the side of the house. Sending Helen back to bed, I sit on the living room couch keeping vigil for the rest of the night, as though that action alone could keep us safe.

Like blazing stars, we claim a bit of land as our own. We decorate it with our homes and gardens, but we are no more in charge than the flowers. We can put up riprap, stone, and wood barriers only to have everything swept away.

27

The Buzz

Dotty

SEPTEMBER 2002

On a mid-September morning, seven months after my optic neuritis and MS diagnosis, I wake at 4 a.m., my left leg asleep. Jonathan's light breathing merges with the hum of early morning cicadas. I really need to pee. Shaking my foot does not make the sharp tingling go away, so I give up, limp to the bathroom, and return to bed. Oddly, the pain in my leg, rather than diminishing, gets stronger. Sleep eludes me. I get up at 5:30.

In the hot shower, my left arm and hand also tingle and buzz. I nod. MS.

During the morning lecture in biology class, when I raise my left arm to point to the diagram I've drawn to explain the details of cellular respiration, my hand flings out of control, slamming into the chalkboard. That's different, I think, lowering my arm, hoping my students didn't notice its spastic behavior.

After lunch, for my environmental science class, I load a school van with equipment: buckets, sieve nets, tubs, waterproof identification sheets, and rubber boots. We drive to our study stream eight miles away and clamber down a slope to wade into the riffles and dip for insect larvae. Depending on the numbers and kinds we find, we can assess the stream's health.

It's a beautiful day, one year and one day since the attack on the World Trade Center and Pentagon. We all have felt a bit anxious, wondering if there will be an anniversary attack. Last September 11th is so vivid in me: being told by the math teacher that a plane had crashed into the first tower; telling my ninth-grade class what I knew; watching the girl in the back row raise her hand and ask, "Do you think anyone was hurt?"

The upper school faculty and students convened in the meetinghouse that day, several students in tears because cell phones weren't working, and they couldn't get in touch with parents who worked in or near the Pentagon. Later, when I used a landline to call Jonathan at his office, and Ruth and Helen at home—I'd learned that Annapolis students had been dismissed early—no one answered. Anxiety, disbelief, fear—no one knew how this could happen, or what was next. I watched my students' faces, hugged them as they cried, and silently vowed to keep them safe, to stay by their side.

Now I pray I can keep that vow.

Scuffling through the stream, elbow-to-elbow with my environmental science students, I realize my right leg also buzzes, and I can't feel the bottoms of my feet. A wide band encircles and squeezes my midsection, as though wrapped like a mummy. I say nothing but instead delight in the students' finds as they strain the water for macroinvertebrates.

Water striders skim across the surface as we collect and count the larvae of mayflies, stoneflies, and dobsonflies. My favorites are the caddisfly larvae, which encase themselves in little homes made of surrounding materials—tiny bits of gravel, sticks, or leaves.

The first one I ever found was with Patty when we were six years old and tramping about in a swampy area we frequented close to our home in South Dartmouth, Massachusetts, a place we called The Sewer. It looked like a two-inch-long log cabin with a little black face peeking out. Having no idea what animal made its own miniature house, nor did my parents, I took it in a jar of water to my first-grade teacher. Shockingly, she could not answer my question. I promised myself that someday I would learn what it was. So much in this world I wanted to know.

Now, my body has even more to teach me.

28

Someone Who Cries

Dotty

SEPTEMBER–DECEMBER 2002

How do they still work? I ponder, as my blue jean-covered legs trudge upstairs after breakfast. My legs feel like those little peanut butter-filled pretzels, but the peanut butter has vanished, leaving hollow pretzel-skinned stumps. I grimace at the intense pins-and-needles-feeling invading my entire left side and right leg, a torturous sensation I call "the buzzies." Tight bands squeeze my legs and abdomen—the MS hug. The bottoms of my feet are numb. My left hand aches sharply. These jeans are killin' me, I think, peeling them off and pulling on a light skirt instead. Dressing for school each day has become a challenge—I cannot stand to be touched. On the way to the car, I grab my cane. Dizziness plus stiffness in my knees have forced me to use it when walking any distance around campus.

Last weekend, to cheer me up, Jonathan took me out in the kayak. I sat in the bow and tried to paddle, but after a few minutes, my left hand hurt too much to grip the shaft. I rested the paddle on the gunnels and tried to keep my voice even as I asked Jonathan to take me back to shore. The distress I felt was not the pain in my hand. It was the anguish in my soul.

As in February after the first MS attack, I've been injecting the three-day course of steroids at night and will go through the month-long taper of prednisone. September is warm in Annapolis, so Ruth and Helen have fashioned a cuff—yellow with a lion face, from a pair of their little girl socks—to cover and hide the PICC line so I can go back into the classroom each day.

Whenever challenges arise in my life, I buck up. Deal with whatever I have to do. I am not someone who cries.

At least I didn't use to be.

For a month now, the full-body buzzing has been constant. Only when first waking in the morning is it gone. Then I get out of bed.

On this rainy October morning, eating the gluten/dairy-free pancakes Jonathan has made for me, my mood is as dark as the sky, and tears cover my cheeks. Each time I bend my head, intense shock waves sear down my arms and burn into my hands, down the backs of my legs into my feet. The crashing harshness of this newest symptom, Lhermitte's Sign, makes me discover how often I bend my head, how often I look down. Jonathan has already helped me wash my hair in the shower. Raising my arms and tipping my head to rinse out the shampoo is excruciating. And hot water exacerbates the pain.

MS symptoms worsen with heat. Before MRIs, doctors diagnosed MS by putting patients in a hot bath. If their symptoms intensified, MS was a likely cause.

The cervical collar my neurologist recommended as a solution—or at least as a reminder not to tip my head—gets strapped on. I wear it while driving but not at school.

Lunchtime finds me eating at my classroom desk instead of crossing campus to the dining hall. Any movement escalates the sensations, and I have to get through my afternoon classes. The weekend is coming, two days of rest. To conserve energy, I've stopped going to Quaker meeting for worship on Sundays, justifying it to myself because I attend meeting with my students at school. Sometimes, Jonathan and the girls go on outings without me. I cry as soon as they leave, a five-minute pity party for the unfairness of it all.

On too many predawn drives to school, I cry, not knowing how to keep going with this exhaustion. Dream of a good excuse to quit, like blindness. The thought, I hate my life, arises unbidden, a shocking realization but a true one. Then the face of one of my ninth-grade boys appears and his smile gives me the impetus to keep driving. But the strain shatters me.

I cry every Sunday night, wondering how to make it to Friday. As the semester continues, too many early mornings find me calling the school. "I am so sorry, but I can't make it today," I say, struggling to hold it together. Deep breaths hold off the tears, and my bed offers comfort. I just can't believe it won't get better. I am a teacher. I am supposed to be teaching.

Upon seeing me, friends often offer the same refrain: "You look great!" Inwardly, I cringe and feel the grimace of every person with MS or other hidden disease. The greeting happens so regularly, it's a joke on MS websites.

But as all those with hidden diseases know, it's a different story inside. It's lonely.

Only I know how intense the nerve pain, how shocking the sensations, how relentless the buzzing, how ever-present the fatigue. Only I know the effort it takes to be okay. Okay for students, for colleagues, for family, for friends. But I am not okay. It will get better, friends say. And day by day, hour by hour, minute by minute, I wait.

How am I supposed to keep doing this? Rest, they say. Right. After an hour commute, I teach, prepare classes, and grade papers from 8 to 3:00. But after-school faculty meetings are out. I stayed once and cried for forty minutes on the drive home because nothing was left inside. Arriving home at 4:15, my body wants to crash. But there's Ruth and Helen, and I want to spend time with them. And with Jonathan. But I am so tired. And there's schoolwork, always schoolwork.

On this December morning, I look in the mirror after brushing my teeth and am mildly astonished to see myself. The flesh remains whole, outwardly there is no change, but inside, I wither. How can I still look and sound like me when so much has faded away?

At school, before classes, while chatting with my biology teacher colleague, I feel separate from myself. My edges smile, talk, and banter, but the rest of me is far away. All that is left is a shell.

29

The End

Dotty

APRIL 2003

The tropical sun heats my outstretched legs as one man after another belly flops into the cruise ship's pool. Each belly-reddening splash makes me cringe, but the crowd cheers as they emerge, whooping and victorious. Frivolous entertainment. Perfect escape. If only this sense of release would last.

Underneath these trappings of vacation and delight, mourning envelopes me.

Two weeks of rest during school's winter break did nothing to abate my depletion. Determined not to abandon my students, I pushed against the wise counsel of faculty mentor Nancy Preuss and vowed to keep teaching until June. But my underlying determination swarmed with tentacles of doubt. June was so far away.

Too far. In late January, my students' jovial demeanors turned to stunned silence when I broke the news. I would be leaving in three weeks, on February 14, Valentine's Day.

Knowing devastation might consume me, I called my college friend Elaine in Atlanta. "I'm going to need you when I stop teaching. Can we get together? Where should we meet?"

"Let me think a minute," she'd said. Half an hour later, she called back.

"There are some good last-minute vacation deals. How do you feel about a cruise?"

Valentine's Day—how ironic. That drizzly cold February day should seem far from this vivid Caribbean Sea, but it sits close, the melancholy passenger I want to avoid but who keeps finding me, sitting too close.

Jonathan drove me to work that day. Though fully capable of driving to school, I just wasn't sure how I could drive away.

After the first classes, I joined the high school students, faculty, and administrators in the meetinghouse for the bi-weekly meeting for worship, the custom in most Quaker schools. It was cold—the heat had just been turned on—and we huddled in coats and mittens on the dark wooden benches, settling in.

A new teacher spoke out of the silence.

"My classroom is down on the ninth-grade wing," he said, "and during the first weeks of school, I often heard the students complaining about Dotty and her biology class. 'It's impossible,' they said. 'Why do I keep getting such bad grades on lab reports? She's too picky.' And I was glad I was not working them that hard. They seemed to like me and my class. Then, as the semester went by, I heard them talking about all they were learning. Details about photosynthesis I'd never heard of. They proudly showed me lab books with A's, B's, congratulatory comments. And I realized that being a teacher is not about making it easy for students; it's not about having them like you. It's about pushing them and helping them reach their potential. To give them the self-confidence to work hard and discover they have more in them than they know. Though I hardly ever see Dotty since she's over in the Bio lab, she has been my mentor. She has taught me how to be a good teacher."

Surprised and touched by his words, I smiled, but my heart felt so heavy. This is the last time I will sit here among these friends, I thought. How can I be leaving? No, don't cry. Take a deep breath. Open my heart.

I waited, eyes closed. Memories flowed in.

Several years ago, a realization struck me. I didn't seem to be someone who would enact big-picture change. Someone who would run a nonprofit, become mayor, work for peace in the Middle East. Deeming this a personal flaw, I called this failing my "Quaker guilt." Many Quaker friends were activists, doing good work to make the world a better place. What was I doing?

Last year, a tenth grader came to my Biology 1 class from another school. "I just want to let you know," she'd told me on the first day, "I hate science. Have always hated it. I thought you should know." I'd said, "Okay. Well, let's see what happens." She became one of my most dedicated biology students, and this year, as an eleventh grader, was taking AP Chemistry.

My style differed from my activist friends who could work on a grand scale. I worked best one-on-one, student-by-student. Perhaps that was enough.

Then, a bubble of happiness welled up. How I have loved working at Sandy Spring. What a gift this has been, to return to this school to teach again after seventeen years, even for this too-short time. To be part of its magic and work where I have felt supported and could be my whole self, mentally, and spiritually.

Deep in this fullness, I was surprised when the meeting for worship ended early. Then the principal announced a special event. Me.

We settled back into silence. One by one, friends stood. Outpourings of stories and thoughtful words sent laughter and awe flooding through me as I heard of my unexpected impact on many of their lives.

"I hated the first weeks of AP Environmental Science," one senior girl said. "We were out counting weeds, measuring trees, writing impossibly hard lab reports, and I thought—I'm out of here. But there was Dotty, right there beside us. Her enthusiasm was so infectious that I just couldn't quit. I am so glad I hung in there. I will use what I've learned for the rest of my life."

Then Tara, my environmental science student —whose mother Trish Cope and I played sports together at Earlham and worked here as colleagues, and whose grandfather Jim Cope was my beloved college ornithology professor—stood up and spoke. And I felt embraced by my connections to her, by my history with the school, and by all present in the room. I let go and cried, for all I had been given ...for all I was leaving.

All I had poured my heart into was over.

Elaine calls to me, "It's time to go snorkeling!" Always intrigued by this sport, I bounce on my toes in the white sand and stifle giggles as instructors hand out gear and instructions. We flipper-walk into the shallows and swim off to explore.

Elaine laughs at my shouts through the mouthpiece, "Wow, oh wow, oh wow!" The twists and flashes of fluorescent fish mesmerize me: slow giants in azure and gold, slender darters of crimson and silver, twinklers of chartreuse and knockout orange. But weariness creeps in, and too soon, I must swim back to shore. Twenty minutes. Curse my exhaustion. But what a gift. The gift of a lifetime.

30

Now What

Dotty

LATE APRIL 2003

I wait until Ruth and Helen have taken the bus to school, until Jonathan has biked to work. Eat breakfast. Wash up the dishes, sweep the kitchen floor. Climb the stairs to our bedroom.

Deliberate. Steady. It's time.

Cross-legged on the carpeted floor, I open my pain journal—the one I write in when nothing else seems to help—grip a pencil in my fist, and in large capital letters over vast swaths of pages, write the words I want to scream.

I HATE THIS! I HATE THAT I CAN'T TEACH ANYMORE. I HATE THAT I HAD TO LEAVE MY STUDENTS! I HATE THIS. I AM A TEACHER DAMN IT. I'M A TEACHER.

Sobs burst from me for the first time in two months since leaving Sandy Spring. Hard crying. Yelling-pounding-sobbing crying. Thank-goodness-the-windows-are-closed crying. I throw the pencil across the room, bang my fist over and over on the journal pages.

Yet in letting go, shame pours in. Oh, poor you, what do you have to complain about? You have a wonderful husband who has a job, fabulous kids. Stop blubbering. It takes all my will to squelch this taunting beast.

For weeks, I have needed to release this spew from my internal dungeon, but I've been careful to keep it barricaded. To not dive down and open the terrible doors. But suppressing grief, anger, and frustration has also meant quashing every emotion. Any joy feels fleeting—like the darting of tropical fish. Love for my family and friends is there but feels shallow. I've feared breaking even the surface of mourning, so, like a water strider, I've skimmed over it, my every word a fraction of its full meaning, every emotion anemic, pale.

So today I begin to find my way again. To find a way to live with who I have been forced to become. Who am I if no longer a teacher, if I no longer work?

I try to believe the answer isn't nobody.

31

The Bog

Dotty

JUNE 2004

Greenery pours onto the woodland trail leading to the bog in Ossipee, New Hampshire on this June morning. Skirting low wet places, I brush past high-bush blueberries, the ripening fruits blushing blue-pink; past stalks of rushes sporting feathery blossoms; past the wildflower surprise of swamp candles—spikes of lemon starbursts with garnet necklaces; through scratchy branches of gnarled black spruce, making me wish I'd worn long pants.

A sandy rise offers the pink blossoms of sheep laurel and spreading bracken ferns, which prefer this drier hummock. I spend a moment here, gazing over the expansive wetlands to the dusky green horizon of spruce and fir and hints of blue-gray mountains beyond. The light whoosh of traffic from the two-lane road seems to belong to another place as I descend to soft peat, tightrope-walk a fallen log, and emerge onto the bog.

Rich reds and greens of sphagnum mosses combine to create the carpet before me. Squatting to look at its intricacies, I find ruby-colored sundews, miniature rosettes with glue-tipped tentacles. Tiny cranberry leaves decorate three-inch stalks, their crimson shooting-star flowers nodding in the light breeze. Waxy-leaved shrubs—leatherleaf and bog laurel—vie for space on this undulating mat.

Life is not easy here. Formed when the glaciers receded, these isolated New England ponds stagnated, their waters low in oxygen and high in acid. Most fish cannot survive and animals are scarce. But well-adapted plants thrive, having evolved mechanisms that allow them to find nutrients in this barren land.

The sundews' glittering nectar has seduced tiny doomed flies. Other hapless insects, lured by scent, perch precariously on the lips of pitcher plants' deep-green troughs before falling into the soup of raindrops and dew where they'll drown in waves of digestive enzymes. All around me, the tiny yellow flowers of horned bladderwort tremble lightly on delicate green stems, belying the hidden underwater network of hair-trigger traps poised to suck passing zooplankton into their chambers.

I take photo after photo with my small point-and-shoot camera. Photographing wildflowers and identifying them has fed my need to learn about the natural world. Finding them fills me the way birds fill me. Fuel for the path ahead.

Every bouncing step sets the mat in motion. The acidic water allows little decay, so soil does not form; only the interwoven roots and rhizomes of these low carnivorous plants and mosses hold this floating mass together. Proceeding gingerly, I listen to squeaks and gurgles as my weight displaces the water, forcing it into new spongy places or squirting out into the pond. One misstep could plunge me into the waiting depths.

I am adapting to my new challenging conditions, though, unlike these plants, I have not been granted the luxury of evolutionary time. Like all whose bodies have gone awry, I've been forced to step carefully or sink.

Over a year of rest has allowed me to emerge, wondering where to go next. Slow walks in the woods and short kayak trips keep me going, though I continually mourn the loss of my students.

Stillness settles on the bog. A goldfinch dips by; a song sparrow ventures a brief solo; a tiny common yellowthroat announces his claim. These moments of birdsong erupt, then disappear into a pervasive hush, a feeling both otherworldly and sacred.

I am living in the midst of a calm—my MS has been in remission for over a year—and bask in a body that still works. My emotions rest lightly on this veneer and most days proceed evenly. But the slightest fright can cause a mushroom cloud of hormonal panic, leaving me exhausted and embarrassed by its inappropriateness. Though my eyes have improved and the intense buzzing has ebbed, twinges, tingles, and numb spots remind me that my central nervous system has been altered and possible new symptoms could appear anytime. As with bladderworts, most are hidden below the surface. I appear fine, even when neurons are misfiring. Upon meeting me, kayaking, or walking with me, you would not suspect disease. With my family's support, I have made adaptations and kept going. Most of the symptoms have been manageable. All but one.

Fatigue. Hard to explain, harder to understand, impossible to measure. Insidious and unpredictable. This is my undulating mat.

As I venture out onto the bog, the stillness is pierced by a sense of unease that seeps through me as the breeze picks up. The sky darkens and thunderheads tower above the pond. Mosquitoes discover me, and their constant whine adds to my unrest. Looking across the sparkling water, I know the gathering clouds could bring a downpour at any moment, with accompanying lightning and hail. Such warnings are not available with MS; I do not know what form my next neurological storm will take, nor when it will arrive.

Though the first raindrops begin to fall, the orchids inspire me to linger. The grass pinks are stunning, dotting the red and green landscape with fuchsia. I photograph as many as the bog permits, hoping to carry home a bit of their grace. A thin area gives me pause, but a hint of white in the leatherleaf border at the pond edge of the bog promises another orchid. Overcoming my trepidation and stepping quickly, I find solid footing and push aside the shrub's tough leaves to reveal their secret. A rose pogonia gleams, flawless in its fringed beauty. Pale pink propellers with a butterscotch tongue tucked inside a peppermint candy lip.

Though my days lack a solid feel of assurance, I walk forward, stepping lightly, balancing energy that can so quickly seep away. I keep my eyes open for orchids, for they are my redemption, my prize for walking the mat of fatigue. Beauty pulls me from my bed each morning, holding its promises just far enough away to keep me moving, seeking its reward.

PART 2

we meet

32

We Begin

Dotty

November 2004

Janet lifts her face to the sun. Her paddle rests on the gunwales of my kayak as we wend our way through Harness Creek, the small tributary behind her house that leads to the South River and the Chesapeake Bay.

From the bow seat, she radiates ease. I maneuver us along the forested shoreline, past the fading yellows of beech and hickory, the reds of maple and dogwood. Only a handful of brown leaves float beside us. Having grown up in southeastern Massachusetts, I am always surprised how late the foliage remains on the trees here in Annapolis.

Janet reaches under her life preserver and zips up her pale pink fleece then pulls her knit hat over her ears despite the unseasonal warmth of the day. She's as thin as the reeds that line the marsh.

"Look," Janet whispers as she points to a pair of hooded mergansers, delightful small hammerhead-crested birds I always hope to find when out paddling. We watch in silence as he raises and lowers his white crest—so striking against his black body—and bobs his head to the female, who raises her soft frosted brown crest in return. Trying not to disturb their courtship, which will last until spring when she lays her eggs, we sneak away, then laugh in unison when a group of small round-bodied bufflehead ducks leaps forward and dives. "Buffleheads are one of my favorites," Janet says. "Mine too!" I reply. Fish crows croak *uh-uhn* to one another from somewhere in the woods; a Carolina wren fusses in the holly. We chat about our kids, the birds, and her neighbors, our conversation as light as the barely-there breeze.

We don't know each other well. Though Stephanie has been in my Girl Scout troop along with my two daughters for the past five years, Janet's and my early time together has been brief, typically a quick greeting when she picks up Steph from meetings and events. This is our first outing together. Janet made it happen.

"Why don't you launch your kayak in the creek behind my house," Janet said to me at a cookie booth after I had regaled her with my love of paddling. "You have to watch the tides—at low tide, the water is too shallow. But you are welcome any time."

"I would love to," I replied, then added with a grin, "but you should come with me."

Her lopsided mouth smiled, her lip pulled up on the left side. I knew she was dealing with oral cancer, but everything seemed to be under control—she told me she'd been on Prinomastat, an experimental drug—and her facial changes seem mild to me. She has lacked the energy to take trips with the troop, but she generously donates snacks—chips, cookies—for our camping adventures and meetings. Her thank-you notes at the end of the year bear heartfelt messages; her thoughtful gifts, pretty and useful. With each offering, she adds, "I wish I could do more."

Her self-consciousness about her face has made her hesitant to be in public. But every fall, when I ask for volunteers, Janet puts aside her inhibitions and, for Steph, works at our Girl Scout cookie booths. She collects money from the girls who cajole the customers into tasting the newest cookie sample before asking if they'd like to buy Thin Mints or Samoas. One year, at a booth outside a grocery store, my two troops—elementary school Juniors and middle school Cadettes—had combined, resulting in four young giggly girls with one older girl who was not very happy to be there without her friends. Janet, recognizing the older girl's discomfort, slipped into the store, then came out and discreetly handed her a rose. A small gift, an offering of compassion.

Today, Janet and I revel in the calm of this early winter day until the setting sun and falling tide send us back to her dock. After I load the kayak on top of my car, we hug and promise each other we will do this again soon.

The nerve endings around my midsection and down my legs buzz from exertion, my core filling with exhaustion. "I can do this," I say as I drive, but my promise to Janet fuels my trepidation. Am I setting myself, and Janet, up for failure? Will I be able to follow through, or will I once again have to disappoint someone by saying no?

33

Journals

Janet

NOVEMBER 2004

A week after the kayaking trip, Janet's doorbell rings, and she jumps up from the couch. "Woody, you don't have to bark," she says, ruffling his shaggy head as she hustles down the hall. Even after two years, Janet misses Dan and the way he and Woody would rush in tandem to the door. Dan died at only seven years old, filled with cancer.

"Dotty! Hi! Come on in."

"I brought you flowers. It always makes me happy when Jonathan brings me cut flowers, so I thought you might enjoy them, too."

"Oh, thank you," Janet says, hugging me. "Yes, flowers always cheer me up. Let me put them in water." Cradling the cellophane cone of maroon and orange chrysanthemums, she bustles into the kitchen.

"You can sit there if you like," she says, pointing to one of the gray sectional couches in the family room. "Then you can put your feet up and be comfortable."

Low sun slides through the glass door. Yellow leaves cling to the trees in her wooded backyard; a blue jay calls with high sharp whistles, imitating the local red-shouldered hawk.

We chat in the eager way new friends do, discovering similarities. Our bond strengthens as we learn we both grew up by the water, swam and goofed around with sisters, plus boated and fished with grandpas.

"My sisters and I were real tomboys," Janet says. "Our whole neighborhood on Long Island was boys, so I'm so glad our mother didn't make us act feminine because we would have had no one to play with. My dad would drive us over to the fish place in East Islip where they'd be cutting off the heads and throwing them in big barrels. We'd send Donna in because she was the youngest, and she'd hang over the barrel on her belly, half-in and half-out, collecting fish heads. We'd go home, jump on our bikes, and go crabbing. You couldn't live on Great South Bay without crabbing.

"We loved it all, crabbing, clamming, plus fishing for blowfish, snappers, and blues. We went to the causeway bridge for snappers, then we'd go home and set up in the backyard, take their heads off, gut them. We started fishing when we were young. I can't remember not doing it."

"Oh Janet, you reminded me of a time Patty and I went crabbing. We brought them home and set them on the floor to see what our cats thought about them, and the crabs scuttled behind the stove. We had to use a yardstick to get them out."

Laughing, Janet adds, "As we got older, Donna teased me. I liked to look nice and might change my clothes three or four times a day, but she'd only change hers every four days. She said I monopolized the washing machine."

More laughter, both of us enjoying this newfound sense of childhood camaraderie.

"I brought you something else, Janet," I say as we're comfortably visiting. I thought you might like a journal. I don't know if this works for you, but I've always found that writing helps me sort out my thoughts. A place to get out all my worries and pissed-off-ness that I won't share with anyone."

Janet sighs. She shakes her head, then nods, both movements almost imperceptible. Her voice is quiet.

"Thank you. I wish I could keep a journal but it's difficult. I jot notes and it helps me feel better to write, but I'm afraid someone might read it and get sad. It's so depressing. No one wants to read that. When I do write something, I just end up throwing the notes away."

We both are silent. To break the unease, Janet picks up a glass of ginger ale to sip through the plastic straw, hoping it doesn't spill down her chin.

"I get almost all my calories this way, my exciting liquid diet."

"Have you ever tried smoothies?"

"No. I've heard of them, but never had one."

"What flavors do you like?"

"I love peach and apricot. I used to eat all kinds of berries, but now the seeds bother me."

"Okay! I have to go pick up Ruth at crew practice, but I'll be back soon."

During our visit, Janet felt a sense of ease, comfort, and calm descending into her core. She has always known when she could trust someone, when a person made her feel like herself—the one inside, behind her scarred face. I hope this friendship works out, Janet thinks, alone now in the family room. It makes me forget about things when we're together.

There's plenty she would like to forget.

"No," she says so loudly that Woody cocks his head at her. She studies a printed email from a sheaf of papers. "They want me to do chemo again. No, no, no!" Dotty's journal is too pretty for what she wants to say. In Reid's room, she finds a discarded composition book whose black-and-white cover has been layered with shiny army tank stickers. "This journal I can write in," she says. "This feels like war."

11/12/04:
Day after my sister Don's birthday
    Yes! I will write as thoughts come to me. I read a response from Dr. Peabody one minute ago—he talks of chemo—"no way, no more!" I say.
    More pain (not just physical) than gain. My last chemo was pointless and useless.
    Last chest x-ray showed 2 lesions on lung (surprise), so must go for Bone Scan, head

to toe, to check for cancer in bones and PET Scan of chest, head, neck, liver, kidney, etc. to test for cancer lesions there. Radioisotope to infiltrate for 45 min w/no movement at all. Then PET Scan takes over.

Yes, I have a bad feeling. There are 2 metastases of C there, but I disagree chemo will cure it. "No go," I say.

How far does one want to labor, pursue travel, suffer, hurt, 'whatever,' before one wants to say, "Enough—no more—I've done what I think I can."

Here I am living w/oral C for 16 years— can't eat, talk, chew, swallow...mouth won't work. Embarrassing to be w/ people.

Absolutely every event has a coffee hour, breakfast, lunch, dinner, etc. Enough of food.

Janet then adds a prayer to Father Francis Seelos, one of the patrons of St. Mary's Church in Annapolis, where he preached in 1862. She and Steve have visited his parish in New Orleans, where he is buried.

Fr. Seelos, from my heart: I never prayed for anything in particular for me—I do now pray for what God and You know I need. C of head, mouth, now lungs (bones, kidney, lungs—it travels and makes you worry.)

I can deal w/it, but I do worry about how my loved ones deal w/it.

"There," Janet says aloud, "I wrote something down." Setting the composition book aside, she picks up her new journal and talks to it. "I'll save you for later. It was nice of Dotty to bring you, but I just can't put all my wretchedness into you." She collects both journals, takes them to her bedroom, and tucks them into a dresser drawer under a neatly folded stack of T-shirts. I hope no one ever reads this, she thinks. Hmmmph. We'll see if I ever write again.

This will be the last time Janet's words find their way into a journal. She will write again, but the next time she puts pen to paper, the circumstances will be quite different.

34

Work

Dotty

May 2005

Sunlight wafts through the waiting room windows and paints the bright blue carpeting. But inside, a familiar shadow creeps as I fill out an annual form for my eye doctor.

How do I negotiate this minefield: Place of Employment, Job Title, Work Phone? What am I supposed to fill in for job title? I sputter to myself. Unemployed? Retired? The dreaded Homemaker?

Everyone my age works. Unlike my mother, who in 1957 at age forty had twin girls and quit her job in the bank trust department because no woman she knew worked after getting married and having children, I had planned to keep working until retirement age. Yet, here I am, forty-eight with no job and my sense of self-worth tied to a paycheck.

Missing the classroom, I tried part-time teaching at a local school, but even one course for one semester proved challenging. Concern about needing to back out of obligations compels me to avoid them: volunteer positions at community centers; bird club outings; committees at our Quaker meeting. My Girl

Scout troop now meets twice a month instead of every week. I attend meeting for worship again, but not regularly, and never stay afterwards to socialize. Being alone doesn't bother me; often, I prefer it though it limits my daily contact with other adults besides Jonathan. Self-checkouts at the grocery store and ATM take less energy than talking.

The hardest part is dealing with the questions and well-meaning advice. What do you do all day? You could work at home on your computer.

Let me make this clear, I want to tell them. I am not an invalid. I walk, do yoga, go kayaking. Watch birds, photograph wildflowers. Sure, rest is necessary, but I am not lazy, and not bored. Stop telling me what job to get. Leave me alone.

I never say these words out loud.

But, in all honesty, I feel lost.

Still plagued by the medical form, I think back to sitting in meetings for worship over the last two years, gathered in communal silence and my own brooding, wondering what I was supposed to do now. An image appeared one week and then showed up for several more weeks. A path, but unlike Robert Frost's roads, neither traveled nor less traveled, but instead, one that felt never traveled. It led into dark woods, where vines would twirl and grasp at my feet, and thorny branches tear at my arms until I had to open my eyes to firmly place myself back in the meeting room. Why was I bushwhacking through this thick brush? What did this image mean?

Then one Sunday meeting, after about a year, the thicket became a line, a straight line as if drawn with a black marker, but with a jagged scrawl off to the left with definite ups and downs. What was this, some strange metaphor for my life? Each time it showed up, I would hold it in the silence and wonder at it. But no answers as to its meaning ever came.

Meanwhile, what I've been doing for solace has become my first step toward direction. Most days, or whenever I feel blue, a walk in the woods or a paddle on the Bay helps. While out there, jotting thoughts and descriptions of what I've seen and heard onto scraps of paper comes naturally. Some of these musings get cobbled into essays. When Jonathan suggested writing one for the *Bay Weekly*, a local paper that publishes reflections, I found the courage and sent one in. The editor accepted that first essay, then a second. Exciting, but today, it still feels so new.

Looking back at the form, do I dare put Writer under the Job Title? I stare at the line and sigh. I check Unemployed.

A word skulks in the back of my mind: worthless. My family needs me, but what am I contributing to the world? Even to my small corner of it?

Appearing lazy distresses me. My sister and I grew up knowing what it was like to work, to do chores at our house and for our grandparents: wash windows, rake leaves, shovel snow, vacuum, dust, haul brush, mow the lawn, wash the car, wash the dishes, weed the garden, harvest apples and peaches to sell by the road, husk corn, dig potatoes. As adults, we both wear that ethic like a pair of coveralls. If something needs to be done, we are the women to do it.

As an athlete, I never was satisfied, pushing harder every day, expecting more of myself every season. Being strong, tough, and capable of whatever the sport demanded was critical; my teammates relied on me. My mantra: Never let anyone down.

Being with students delighted me, whether in the classroom, on the playing field, in the gym, or in wilderness areas. When people asked about my job, I answered with pride: I teach.

Now, I must sit down. Must lie down. Must say no, I can't.

Hearkening back to that moment on Southwest Field Studies in Big Bend National Park when I knelt to rub an Earlham friend's shoulders, I realize how much better I've become at reaching out to others, talking with them, listening. I am really good at listening. But only marginally better at listening to myself, to my body's pleas. It's too discouraging to accept what I hear. My truest heart is still in hiding. Opening to its voice means also opening to my sorrow of losing who I was. That's a sorrow so deep it scares me.

I never feel someone else is less worthy because they do not work. Certainly not Janet. She is no less worthy of respect, love, and happiness, no less important to the world. Yet I do not afford myself the same consideration.

What am I good at now? What can I do? Back in November, a couple of days after promising to return, I went to Janet's with fruits and yogurt and made her a peach smoothie. She sipped a little, proclaimed it delicious, but left most of it. Was it too thick, or was she not hungry? I didn't ask but drove home feeling inadequate to the task of being Janet's friend. Would anything I do possibly make a difference?

As we sat on her couches that day, Janet had mentioned her own feelings of inferiority. She lamented her lack of energy to do all she wished she could. "Look at me. I just sit here." Though we could commiserate on some levels, Janet was dealing with so much more than I.

Now, six months later, while I've been bemoaning what box to check, Janet is figuring out how to stay alive.

35

Wounds

Janet

JULY 2005

Janet can't stop her heart from racing. She tries taking deep breaths, but that only seems to exacerbate the pounding. Pain pulses through her face, a drumbeat sounding a message she's afraid to hear. She prays this new doctor will have an answer. Prays there will be some hope. Prayers sustain her; what else does she have?

She clings to the deep spiritual grace she felt in Garabandal, the tiny miracles of the fork and the pine cones. But too often, she feels abandoned and alone.

How many days has she hidden in her bedroom, curled under the covers, willing death? I am no good for anyone, anyway, she'd think. It just hurts so much. I can't take it. Death at least will release me.

She sits on the molded plastic seat next to Steve in the exam room, her slender hand in his warm grip.

"So what if the news is bad this time," she quips to Steve. "Are we going to sail around the world? Or if it is good, are you going to build me another boat?" Her words belie her nerves, which shudder through her belly. Her jaw shivers.

"Honey," Steve says, "I will go anywhere, build anything, do whatever you want forever and ever. I just hope this doctor can give us some direction."

Janet looks at the dark smudges under his eyes. She knows he's tired. Knows he had another migraine yesterday. When will this end? she thinks. How will it end? I just can't stand the idea of leaving Steph and Reid. And how can I ever leave Steve? She shakes her head, trying to banish the deep sadness that blooms, again.

The waiting seems interminable. Deep in the convoluted hallways and offices of Johns Hopkins University Hospital in Baltimore, they've come to the one doctor other oncologists have recommended.

Janet's stock-piled stash of the drug Prinomastat, which has kept her tumors at bay for seven years, has run out. The drug company has stopped making it. Steve has persevered in his research trying to learn more about how adenoid cystic carcinoma invades the body, what oncologists are saying, what trials are underway. Developing his own hypotheses. Searching for any clues. But he's found no answers yet.

Janet glances around the sterile-looking white room and reads a cancer poster: *Healthy eating, physical activity, and being lean reduce the risk of the most common kinds of cancer that affect women,* it states.

Yeah, she scoffs, if only that worked for uncommon cancer. But hey, who am I kidding. Can't eat, can hardly exercise—but guess I got the lean one right. Too right. I'm practically invisible.

She lets out a sigh, but every breath she takes feels strained. Nervous waves continue their agitated romp through her core.

A brisk knock makes Janet jump. She sits up straight, watching the oncologist stride in. A clearly pregnant oncologist.

"Hello, Janet," she says. "And you must be Steve.

"Well, let's get this over with. I looked at your chart, Janet. Your cancer has metastasized. There are now two tumors in your lungs. The tumors in your head and neck are growing, and tumors have returned to the original site in your sinus cavity.

"Janet, let's face it, you have adenoid cystic carcinoma. It is unheard of that you have survived this long. There are simply no drug trials or other treatments beyond what you have already done. I can't prescribe anything, and surgery is too risky. There is nothing left to do. I have nothing to offer."

And with that verdict, she turns and walks out.

On the drive back to Annapolis, Janet stares out the front window. The nervous shudders are gone, but so is everything else. She feels hollow. A broken shell cast onto an empty beach. The words *I have nothing to offer* keep repeating in her head.

She does not see Steve's rigid jaw, nor his pale knuckles as he squeezes the steering wheel in his fists.

"I guess this is it," Janet says, still staring straight ahead, stifling a sob. "It's over. But, Steve—she didn't even say she was sorry. Couldn't she at least have said she was sorry?"

"Jan!" Steve says, his voice furious. "How many doctors have we run into that have been wrong? Plus, that woman is a cyborg! She is not even a human being. If she were a human being she would have done something, she would have emoted, she would have given you some support. I don't even know how a pregnant woman can be so devoid of feelings. She's wrong, Jan, she's wrong. We will find someone else. We will find an answer. Trust me, Jan. She is wrong. It is not over."

Janet takes a deep breath, releasing it in a long sigh. She curls into a tight ball and covers her face with her hands. Pulses of pain radiate behind her eyes, around her jaw. She feels encompassed by it, beaten up by it. Pummeled and left to bleed—by a doctor.

Some wounds never heal.

The next day, Janet slips a note, written on purple teddy bear notepaper, into Steve's lunch bag:

> *Want to know how much I love you?*
> *See the width of my arms? No.*
> *—Cause it's infinite—*
> *I'm sorry I'm so bad to (or for) you & R & S.*
> *Love you*
> *J*

Steve replies in a long letter:

> *...the love I feel for you is the source of my greatest joy...and lately my greatest pain...*
>
> *I need you to tell me what to do. You know that I'll do anything to keep you here and will gladly accept any consequences that may bring. No matter how many challenges you may face, I'll gladly face them with you, just to keep you here.*
>
> *But I don't want to cause you any more hurt. If you really don't want to fight anymore, I will honor your decision. I won't like it. I won't agree with it. It will be the hardest thing I'll ever do. But I'll honor your decision, whatever it may be.*

36

Pre-op Paddle

Dotty

SEPTEMBER 2005

I lower my kayak off Janet's dock into water tinged brown after runoff from recent rains. Around us, red-winged blackbirds squeak, pipe, and whistle from the phragmites on this balmy afternoon. Though I hold the kayak steady, Janet hardly needs my help. With the confidence of a lifetime boater, she steps in and sits in the bow seat, trim in tan capris, sun hat, and life jacket over white shirt, camera hanging around her neck. No need to hand her a paddle. Her light weight makes it easy for me to manage the boat myself.

Pushing off, I aim us down the left side of Harness Creek, where branches of sycamore, oak, sweet gum, and holly shade us with lush greens. A pair of mallards preens on a partially submerged log.

At the first bend, Janet points out a friend's dock where Steve keeps another boat. I wonder how many boats they have, and if Steve made them all, but don't ask.

"Gloria and Johnny are the best neighbors," she says, laughing. "I hope you can meet them someday. Their stories always crack me up."

I learn of the special bond between Janet and Johnny. Because of his own cancer, Johnny's tongue has been removed.

Skimming along the shady edge of the creek, we watch black swallowtail butterflies dabbling in wet sand, migrating monarchs winging their way south, and a blue-and-white belted kingfisher zipping from bank to bank, his raspy cries rattling the afternoon hush. We pause, soaking in these wild things. Each sighting feels like a release from all that is not right here, right now.

We reach a cove tucked away from the chop on the South River. The dry leaves of phragmites rustle; the bushy groundsel trees blossom in white clouds of fluff. Trees soar above us and surround us, offering a sense of sanctuary. We chat, rest. Stillness envelops us. Every branch is mirrored, a single cloud floats below, a lone osprey circles overhead. We hear the plop-splash of a fish jump behind us, then only the drone of crickets. Janet's ribs expand as she takes long breaths of the late summer air. Catching her breath recently has not been easy.

At an evening Girl Scout meeting two days before, Stephanie handed my co-leader and me a note.

I've been wanting to touch base and say Hi, Janet's note said, *but things have been getting out of control (cancer-wise). I'm going to Beth Israel Hospital in New York for major, major surgery on October 5th.*

We read about the spread of the cancer, and how Steve's research this fall has led them to a reconstructive team who feels confident they can surgically remove the tumors in her face and also save her left eye. *We'll see about that,* she wrote. She'll be in New York for two weeks; recovery will take four to six months. She and Steve told Steph and Reid last night.

Steph watched as we read the note. Our eyes met—hers sorrowful and haunted. We shared a long hug.

Janet also mentioned that October 5 is Steve's birthday and that *for the last twenty-three years, I never have been able to give him a party. Something unplanned and uncontrollable always pops up in our lives.*

With Steph's permission, I told the Scouts, who jumped into plans for an early surprise party for Steve. I made different plans. It was time for me to reconnect with Janet after being away too long.

We visited the next day, catching up in her family room. She asked me how Helen was doing at high school, about Ruth's college hopes, what Jonathan had cooked lately, how I've been feeling. I told her I've been working on a quilt.

"I've always wanted to make a patchwork quilt," Janet said, twisting her mouth into a wry smile. "I just hadn't planned to make one with this," she added, pointing to her face. "Are you comfortable hearing about the details?"

I nodded.

"The doctors plan to cut around my skull, under my left eye, then around my nose and mouth," she said, tracing the circuitous route. "Then they will lift back my face to remove the tumors."

I'm not squeamish. I've cleaned teenagers' wounds and splinted their broken bones while backpacking in the wilderness. I've done CPR on a neighbor having a heart attack, and carved embedded cactus spines out of my calf with a Swiss army knife. But this felt visceral. Faces in anatomy books with the flesh removed popped into my mind. Those faces, her face.

"I'm most afraid of the tracheotomy," she said, which surprised me. With all she's about to undergo, a trach seemed negligible. I told her of friends who've recovered with minor scars.

"I know. I've just had so much radiation," she said. "I'm afraid it won't heal."

I silently chastised myself for making assumptions. So much I don't know about what she's been through over the past sixteen years.

We joked about turtlenecks; pondered her elegance with multi-colored silk scarves draped about her throat.

What was there to say to someone who was about to have her face carved as cruelly as a Halloween pumpkin? I reached for words that might hold meaning and convey support without falling into loathsome platitudes, hoping my comments didn't sound too flippant or trivial.

Caught in these thoughts, I was startled when she jumped up.

"I want to show you something," she said. She hustled down the hall then returned with her wedding picture. Her face was flawless. Her peach-tinted cheeks glowed beside her gentle smile, her auburn curls drifted around her shoulders.

"I'm showing the doctor this picture. I want to look like this again."

How could her mangled face be restored: her unblinking left eye, bloodshot and unfocused, bulging with the underlying tumor; the dark purple bruise tucked in a pocket of flesh rimming her lower lid; her mouth unable to open a finger's width; her left lip raised in a perpetual sneer. Her wishes, I suspected, would run aground on this reality. But her sneer wasn't real. I know her kindness.

She told me she'd come to terms with her doubts. Had made the decision to keep fighting, to have this surgery. She was not ready to quit.

What she couldn't acknowledge aloud was the raw trepidation that lives inside her, but her distress was palpable. Her longing was clear when she glanced at her children's photos behind me, when she talked about Steph and Reid. She wasn't done being a mom.

I made a silent vow to keep visiting, to support her as she faced this surgery and whatever came next. A vow, that come what may, I planned to keep.

We could have floated in the Harness Creek cove for hours, but the tide has turned, and low tide means a knee-deep muddy walk to her dock. Energy flagging, I barely dip the paddle as we meander up the creek, the afternoon asking for nothing more. Then we notice a great blue heron on a dead branch overhanging the water.

"I want a picture," Janet whispers.

We edge along, barely breathing. She snaps picture after picture as we slip under the branch. The heron remains motionless, a king surveying his domain. After we pass, he flaps off, uttering his raspy resonant blats.

At the last bend, out of the blue sky, a rain shower patters down. She looks at me and we laugh. Nothing matters right now. Nothing.

37

Nightgowns

Dotty

SEPTEMBER 2005

Janet opens the front door, and we both grin. Hug, look into each other's eyes, laugh, and hug again, delighted to be together. We head to the couches and Janet offers me tea. A bottle of water already sits on the coffee table. We catch up a bit on our children, on daily doings.

Then we launch into the details of her upcoming surgery: the complexities of reconstruction, the many hours under anesthesia, and the complications that can arise from a stomach tube.

"Maybe they'll fatten you up!" I tease.

After an hour, as I am preparing to head home, she clears her throat.

"I know you are busy," Janet says, "but would you be able to slit open the front of my nightgowns and sew on Velcro? The nurses will need access for the feeding tube."

"No problem," I say, but sigh inwardly, wondering how big the job will be and if I can get it done in time. Inside the plastic bag are three pale cotton nightgowns. Buck up, I think. You can handle this. You must handle this.

Kneeling on the floor that evening, I smooth the front of the first nightgown over my cutting board, touch the rotary blade to the fabric, and slice down the center only to stop abruptly. A shiver passes through me. The scalpel, the bright surgical lights, my own anxieties crowd my view. I rock back on my heels and brush away tears. Oh, Janet. Closing my eyes, I take a deep breath, and whisper a prayer. Then, continue to cut.

38

Eye Contact

Janet

SEPTEMBER 2005

Janet needs some potatoes for tonight's dinner. Steve could stop on his way home from work, but she decides she can do it. *I can't hide all the time,* she thinks. She slips on a light sweater and combs her hair—darker now that she's been avoiding the sun—but barely glances in the mirror. After a five-minute drive to Safeway, she walks across the parking lot toward the front door and feels her inner turmoil kick into high gear.

Where do I look? I always used to look at people, nod, say hi, but now I'm so afraid of their eyes. Those looks I get...disgust, surprise, pity...oh God how I hate the pity. That sweet, treacly look that says, oh you poor thing. I just want to smack 'em. Or duck away. But I've got to face people. I hate looking like this. I hate it. I feel like a freak. I'm just me, I want to tell them. I'm still me.

Janet enters through the automatic doors. "Janet!" A grocery clerk rushes out from behind the service counter and embraces her. "It makes me so happy to see you again." They chat, catching up. Her nerves now calmed, Janet pushes her cart toward the produce section.

She selects a bag of Yukon Gold potatoes, then carrots, and a bunch of parsley. They're having pork chops tonight. A homey treat before she and Steve head to New York. A woman edges past a wooden bin of onions and garlic, and Janet looks up.

"Hi," Janet mouths, nodding and smiling at the woman. Then she sees the little girl. Reddish-brown hair, just like mine used to be. The girl hugs a stuffed dog, tawny like Dan, and as Janet opens her crooked mouth to tell her she had a dog like that, the little girl's face convulses.

"Mommy! Mommy! A witch!" the girl cries, clinging and pulling at her mother's sweatshirt.

Janet feels her body melt. The girl's horror jabs her, pierces every veneer she's carefully placed to cover her vulnerability until she feels as though she is caving in on herself. She stumbles toward the door, across the parking lot. Fumbling with her keys, hands shaking, she opens the car door, slumps in, and puts her head on the steering wheel. Her shoulders heave, her whole body rocking in spasms of grief, her breath pulsing in short uneven gasps.

"I can't stand this," she whispers.

39

Trying to Breathe

Dotty

SEPTEMBER 2005

An unexpected sob bursts from me while flipping another pancake; reality dropping through my gut like a stone. Friends my age now get sick, get diseases. Janet faces not only disease, but the possibility of death. Her fears about the surgery resonate as tremors inside my chest. Five days. I hold Janet up to God more frequently now, praying she is not forgotten.

The kayak calls. I hope paddling will clear my head and help quiet my foreboding. Launching into Duvall Creek, I paddle to the cove to check on my favorite wildflowers. Each year, erosion further undercuts the blazing star's grassy bank, diminishing their numbers. I spot their purple stalks but only a dozen remains. Someday they will be gone.

Scratchy squeaks of iridescent grackles patrolling the shoreline add background music, but the gray sky and grayer water of the overcast day reflect my mood. I paddle on through light ripples, riding the swells from distant boats. Twenty resident geese fly over; a handful of mallards scout the shallows. Late

September is quiet here on the Bay, a lull between waterfowl migrations. Ospreys have headed south; tundra swans and sojourning ducks won't arrive for over a month.

The whole Bay sits in front of me, the horizon unclear. Herring gulls flap past; a low-slung workboat glides by. Falling into the easy rhythm of paddling, I let my mind drift, amorphous as the day. Time slips on, my paddle taking me farther than planned, but no destination is far enough. The heaviness remains lodged inside.

Beginning to tire, I know it's time to head back. The breeze picks up, sending a chill through me. I dig in against the choppy waves, jaw set as arms pull-push, pull-push. Muscles burn. But I am strong—I have to be—and keep going.

Arriving at the entrance to Duvall harbor, I stop and float, my wooden paddle across the gunnels. I ease into the backrest and sigh. What was the point? All I've accomplished is wearing myself out.

Below me, billions of phytoplankton cling to life. Diatoms, one-celled jewels of the sea encased in walls of silica glass, whirl in the wind-charged waves as copepods eat them like candy. Dinoflagellates propel themselves with whip-like flagella up toward light or toward prey; they, in turn, are scooped up by zooplankton and small fish. But an overpopulation of these algae results in low oxygen, making it difficult for fish to breathe. Below me, a whole world lives and dies. We are all trying to breathe.

A line lies along my port side, a length of fishing line six inches from my hull. I try to pluck it out, concerned that the birds will get tangled, but my fingers come up empty. I stare, trying to fathom this long thread-like dent, then laugh at myself, at my misreading of the water.

It is a line of calm. A line delineating where the wind and waves approaching on my starboard have been stopped by the presence of my boat. From my hull to the line, the water is glassy and tranquil. Beyond it, riffle and chop.

Exhaling, I stretch my legs and settle into this cushion of quietude. Close my eyes. Let the waves rock me. Halyards clink. Blue jays call from nearby trees. A fish crow squawks.

"You're going to make it, Janet. I know you are going to make it."

The sun, having eluded me all morning, emerges.

40

The Surgery

Janet

OCTOBER 2005

Beth Israel Hospital, New York. Oncology surgery. Thirteen hours. Eight surgeons. Ninety percent of the tumor removed. Ten percent still remains, too close to her facial nerves, carotid artery, the base of her skull.

In the ICU, monitors beep, fluorescent lights pulse, footsteps squeak, voices murmur, ventilators whoosh. Nurses poke the skin grafts bulging in lumpy patches over the left side of Janet's face, check their warmth, check to make sure blood oozes. Check incisions on hip and abdomen where bone and muscle were harvested for her jaw and new palate, now a swollen mass crowding her mouth. Check the nasogastric tube that snakes through her right nostril to her stomach. Check PICC line, trach site, IV levels. Check monitors for blood pressure, heart rate, oxygen level. The monitors beep incessantly, send out alarms. The fluorescent lights pulse, footsteps squeak, voices murmur, ventilators whoosh.

Two days after surgery. Tissue grafts hold. Ventilator is removed. Still uncommunicative after the extensive anesthesia, Janet suddenly pitches and heaves, her arms and legs flail. Restraints are added. Her face bleeds.

Five days after surgery. Swelling recedes, grafted tissues hold but sag in folds, the face of a bloodhound. Nurses talk of move to a step-down unit. Until—mayhem. Incoherent yelling. Fists pummeling Steve, Lynn, anyone in range. Nurses struggle to apply restraints. Heavy sedation.

Emergency CT scan. No neurological irregularities. Doctors chalk it up to ICU: disrupted sleep, medications, overstimulation from bright lights, constant voices, alarms.

Except for sedation, all medications stopped. Twelve solid hours of sleep. Sleep for everyone.

Eight days after surgery. Step-down unit. Quiet. Four rooms, one empty. Conscious now. The NG tube for nutrition remains in place. Tracheotomy still in place. Ear tubes inflamed. Facial swelling precludes glasses. The light feels too bright.

Janet picks up a pen to write, not in a journal this time, but in an old red spiral-bound notebook. Not to record her innermost thoughts, but to communicate with Lynn and Steve.

I just wish I could hear, Janet writes. *Tough enouf not being able to talk but to barely see and not hear is the worst.*

Lynn copies a Jumble from the newspaper into

the notebook in large letters, which Janet solves in a flash. In writing, they pour over the stats of the Yankees' game, discuss how Janet is feeling. Back and forth. The long day putters on.

In the late afternoon, Lynn heads back to a nearby apartment building where rooms are available for the families of patients.

Did Lynn make it back to her room okay? Janet writes to Steve.

She made it fine. However, she was yakking on her cell phone to Charles and ran into a construction pole in front of the Apt. bldg. She said she was so embarrassed. Walking and talking on a cell phone is the best way to look like you're a local NY'er.

Ear concerns. Elevated temperature. Headaches. Hard to talk, to swallow. Janet looks at her face in a handheld mirror, trying to see through the blur. Her tumor-ridden left eye is gone, the eye socket empty, rimmed in dark congealed blood.

A nurse writes, *So, what do you think of your new face?*

Shocked, Janet replies. *My eye is so big and there is nothing there. But I need to see more of it. It's amazing what has been done so far. There is hope.*

Nine days after surgery. Early morning. Her sister Donna arrives for a surprise visit.

If you smell something, it's my feet, Donna writes. *They are wet and cold!*

Great to see you. We can catch up before Steve and Lynn come, but this is the first day I am learning to talk.

They write back and forth until Steve and Lynn return. Then all go over Janet's progress and new looks, her lip much more symmetrical, the skin under her left eye socket now soft and smooth, no longer hard and wrinkled.

Do you remember, Janet writes, *before I knew I would lose my eye, how I teased with you, Donna, that I'm Olive Oyl—bony, and Popeye—lopsided lips/ one eye closed. You know, I still laugh about it but must learn not to say certain things in fun to lighten the load. Fiction might become fact!*

At lunchtime, the joking continues when Donna returns with take-out food for herself, for Steve and Lynn. Janet still cannot swallow.

There's one miracle, Janet writes. *My smell is better. At first, I thought it was Donna's feet, but it's Chinese chicken!*

Later, when Donna gets ready to take the train home, she writes a list for Janet: *Love you lots; See you Saturday; Hope you don't mind I'm leaving but you need to be quiet; And I'm still the pretty one.*

Well, yeah, today I'll give you that one, Janet responds. *Today you are prettier.*

Ten days after surgery. Janet worries about her kids—hopes Reid's college tuition got paid, wonders if Steph is okay home alone with Woody, who apparently is still moping around.

Sitting in the chair next to her bed, Steve catches her up. *The woman we planned to stay with Steph didn't work out, but the neighbors are checking in.*

Dotty took Steph kayaking last Saturday, offered to let her stay at her house while we're here in NY, but Steph told her she's fine with Woody. My mom arrives today to stay with her.

Please get some postcards for Steph, Janet writes back, *so we can send about three a week to her. Tell her how proud we are of her responsibility and maturity. God forbid, I never see her shining eyes again.* She takes a deep breath, lets it out in a long exhale.

I cannot, I will not, Janet thinks, abandon my children.

Steve continues his research, endless calls, and emails to oncologists and other doctors, setting up appointments, determining the next steps. He visits Janet every day and they write in her ever-present notebook about his findings, her needs. One evening just before he heads back to his room, Janet writes:

Please buy a beer so for once you can get home (before you become a pumpkin), enjoy and relax. Please, it would make me so happy. Good nite. Love you madly. It's so joyful when I see you in the morning. J

Bit by bit, Janet makes progress. Three antibiotics clear up the hip infection. Small swallows of water. Trach removed. Ten-minute walks. Stairs conquered. Going to the bathroom involves an actual bathroom. Glasses fit. Finally, she can see.

Seventeen days after surgery. Discharged! Home to Lynn's house. No tubes, no antibiotics. She can now drink liquids and eat soft foods, though her new palate is quite swollen. Swallowing is hard. Talking is difficult. Eating is exhausting. Everything is exhausting, yet Janet remains irrepressible.

"What do you want for supper," Lynn asks Janet who reclines on the couch, one hand lazily stroking Lynn's dog.

Using hand signals, Janet raises her hand toward her mouth as though lifting a cup, waves her hand in front of her face as though she were hot, then with both hands, makes a "T." Her face crinkles in delight.

"Tomato soup!" Lynn laughs. "Coming right up."

41

This Time of Transition

Dotty

OCTOBER 2005

The geese awaken me in the blush of pre-dawn. The staccato echo of their honking resounds through the stillness and I imagine their long lines check-marked across the pale pink sky. These are not resident geese but migrants coming in for the winter. I can hear it in their voices.

I creep out of bed and into fleece clothing. Tying the kayak onto the roof of the car, I drive one mile to the end of our road, where the Chesapeake Bay sits before me. Pulling up to the boat launch on Duvall Creek's sandy spit, I see the sparkling grey-blue harbor and know it'll be a good paddling day. Hauling the kayak off the car and into the shallows, I push off into the barely rippling water, into the perfect blend of sun warmth and breeze cool, giving a wave to the sailor who calls, grinning, "Watch out for the nasty weather!" I find my rhythm and go.

Rusty red and faded gold wash through the trees, though oak, hickory, and maple still hold tightly to their lush canopies. I paddle the edges, where different habitats converge and diverse life flourishes, though the approaching cold lessens the usual abundance.

The red-winged blackbirds no longer sing and contend for territory; the crickets have gone silent as they fall into their winter sleep. Gone are the songs of robins; even the cardinals are quiet now. From the reeds comes a smattering of goldfinches, seed-lovers like the cardinals who will remain through the winter.

All summer and into the fall, these shallows have offered haven for tiny fishes whose sleek shapes dart and hide, then dapple the smooth surface in front of my bow. Steady summer rain kept the salinity low in this northern part of the Bay, and the sea nettles arrived late this year. I recall watching one of these jellyfish as it swayed in the green water in early September, its translucent gelatinous dome accented with milk and peach highlights. Long ghostlike tentacles undulated beneath in a pulsating dance for one.

The last remnants of saltmarsh asters still adorn the grassy shoreline while the fuzzy flowers of the groundsel tree glow in a pearly finale. I paddle alongside to absorb them, to hold them in my memory.

Soon more winter waterfowl will arrive from northern breeding grounds, seeking these warmer waters. I look forward to the hooting chorus of the tundra swans, to the pattering sound of ruddy ducks taking off, to the scattered carpets of canvasbacks and scaup.

I settle into this time of transition and wait for Janet to come home.

Minute to Minute

Janet

OCTOBER 2005

Healed enough from the surgery in New York, Janet arrives home to joyful hugs from Steph, to happy barks from Woody, his tail beating against her legs, a rhythm she has missed. She ruffles his wiggling furry body.

Exhausted from the five-hour drive from Lynn's, Janet collapses onto the couch and sighs. I am so glad to be home, but this pain is the pits.

The incisions on her hip and belly ache, jabbing with sharp twinges every time she moves, a constant reminder of the ravage necessary to put her face back together. Her tongue wanders up to her new palate, still so tender. She touches the lumpy additions to the left side of her face. They feel numb, as though they aren't even part of her.

As days pass, the incisions holding the grafted tissues in place refuse to mend. One open wound becomes three. Prior radiation is slowing the healing, but also, during her seventeen-day stay at the hospital, she contracted MRSA. Methicillin-resistant

Staphylococcus aureus is a bacterial infection renowned for its resistance to antibiotics. By early
November, she's back in the hospital in Annapolis
to receive a strong course of intravenous antibiotics.

Writing to update family and friends, Steve cannot
hide his despair. *Obviously, this is not what we were
looking for. I'm tempted to say, 'What next?' but I fear
that an earthquake will swallow my house or some
sort of similar cataclysm. To say this is a tough road to
walk is a monumental understatement. I used to say
we're taking things one day at a time. Now it's more
like minute to minute.*

Her wounds and infection put her in and out of
Annapolis and New York hospitals as doctors oversee
her recovery. The surgical team at Beth Israel is
pleasantly surprised with her progress despite the
infection; the local Annapolis doctors are concerned.

Steve and Janet find themselves in a quandary:
they want to embrace Beth Israel's outlook but are
wary of the two completely different prognoses. They
decide to go a third route and consult the wound
center at Johns Hopkins.

"I wish this weren't so hard," Janet says to Steve
one night as they spoon under the covers in bed,
Steve's arm curling around her.

"Agreed," he says, his voice weary. "But if there is
anything we've learned, it's not to overreact, whether
the news is good or bad. Let's listen to all the doctors,
then make decisions. We'll just have to see what
Hopkins says.

Janet shifts, trying to find a comfortable position. She glances up at the statue of Mary, barely visible in the dark room, and wonders if this latest surgery had been a mistake. Wonders if Steve would agree. They had weighed all the options beforehand, gone over and over the choices. Should they have tried to find something less invasive? But there was nothing else. It was this or let the tumor win. Was there hope or was this surgery just prolonging the inevitable? But she remembers her absolute clarity when she finally decided to go ahead with the surgery. She wanted to live.

She hears Steve's steady breathing as he slides into sleep, then whispers to herself, "I'm glad I'm still here for Steph and Reid, and for you, Steve. But if it were just me, I think I'd be done."

43

They Sing

Dotty

DECEMBER 2005

I visited during those fall months after Janet returned home. She'd come to the door with her head and face wrapped in a scarf, wondering who was there, worried about their reaction. "Oh, it's you," she'd say, smiling and letting the scarf fall away. We'd hug, then hug again as per usual—our elation at seeing each other too boundless for a single hug—and head to the couches.

Janet and I understand each other. We both agreed when we set up our get-togethers that either one of us could cancel, even at the last minute. Exhaustion often grips Janet now. Sometimes I forget to call before a planned visit and knock for several minutes before giving up and returning home. Later, she'll tell me she was asleep.

Today, Janet and I sit in her family room amidst the fuchsia profusion of ten large flowering Christmas cacti covering the floor in front of the hearth. Janet is chipper; every question I ask leads to a story. She tells me about the woven tree from San Antonio that hangs on its nail on the stonework above the fireplace, as it has every Christmas for the past nine years. About the wooden clogs on the right side of the hearth from Garabandal, which prompt her to jump up in search of a black film canister. She pries off the grey lid, and out tumble tiny pine cones into my hand.

She regales me with the details of her visit to the remote Spanish town: about finding the fork, hearing the wind in the Pines, finding these little cones. Cradling them in my palm, I feel as though I, too, have been blessed.

The sun sits low beyond their fir Christmas tree perched in its stand by the sliding glass doors. Boxes of lights and ornaments sit beneath it; no one has had the time or energy to trim the tree. I fight an inner urge to put them up.

At home, we have just finished decorating our tree, a tall, broad Frasier fir, aglow with a dozen strands of colored and white lights that Jonathan has woven through the branches from trunk to tips. We love Frasier firs because the heavy limbs are spaced apart, leaving room to hang ornaments not just on the branch ends but also deep inside the tree. Hundreds of ornaments—precious ones from Jonathan's and my childhoods, the ones the girls have received each Christmas, the stunning blown glass and intricate wooden ones from our trips to Germany with Jonathan's family, the ones given to us by friends—all have found a home on the tree. Each ornament has a story.

Janet tells me her story of past Christmases, always at her parents' house, even after she and Steve were married. How on Christmas Eve, the cousins would bundle up and gather outside to wait for Little Grandpa to materialize from The Digger as Santa Claus, then stomp from house to house visiting relatives to get a gift or a sugary treat. How she and Steve drove up to East Islip, their car laden with presents and her specialties: key lime pie, sweet potatoes with apples and marshmallows. Boisterous Christmas dinners, the inevitable wrapping-paper fights, the infectious laughter when Janet began her songs, lyrics she would write and sing to the tune of Christmas carols.

In her hoarse voice, she sings one she wrote for her mother last Christmas to Away in a Manger.

"We love you dear Mother, God's gift from above. You're caring, you're giving, you've taught us to love."

Her voice catches. "I never fully appreciated how much my mother taught me," she says, "until I, too, had children."

Then she giggles.

"Oh, what fun I had teasing my siblings, though." Mischief sparkles in her eye. "Ha! I remember one. I sang this to Donna's husband Bob to tease her.

"Oh, I'm a happy boy," she sings to Jingle Bells, "my heart is filled with joy, especially now at Christmas time, when I'll get lots of toys. Now Santa here it comes, I know that I'll be gunned, but all I ever want from life is maybe a new wife, OH!"

Janet rocks with laughter. "Donna was so mad! She barely let me sing the chorus.

"Happy boy, happy boy, happy as can be. Don, I'm only teasing, you're the best wife that could be."

Watching her laugh makes me laugh even harder.

"I'll have to find all the lyrics," she says. "They're around here somewhere. Maybe Lynn has them. Yeah, we had so much fun."

The scars streaking across her left cheek add to her dynamic flare. I'm getting used to her missing left eye. The new normal.

"Did I tell you about the time I tried to feed toast to the VCR?" Janet asks with a grin.

"No..."

"Yeah...a few years after the radiation in San Antonio, I started mixing up words. When asking for a glass of water, I'd say, "Please bring me a chair." And then, when Steve would figure it out and hand me the water, I'd reach for the glass and miss. Doctors found a huge cyst in my brain probably caused by the radiation, so they drained it, and that solved things. Until..."

"What?"

"I began having seizures a few months later. Apparently, I'd stagger around, slur my speech and get all confused, then sleep for several hours and never remember a thing. One day Steve came home and found me trying to fit a piece of toast in the VCR slot. When he asked what I was doing, I told him it was hungry!"

We slap our thighs, laughing ourselves breathless. How good it feels. Our early Christmas present for two.

We hear Steve come in the front door. Woody raises his head in greeting.

"Oh, I forgot to tell you," she says. "I'm on a new drug now. Thanks to Steve."

"Really? What did Steve do now?" I say, smiling at him as he wanders into our midst, gives Janet a kiss.

"He's been doing research," Janet continues, "and over the last year or so has come up with a plan called Pharmacobiotics. After talking with oncology researchers, he and they all decided on this drug I should try."

"Steve," I say, "You're an IRS guy. How did you get to know so much about cancer?"

"Lemme get a beer first and I'll tell you," he says. He grabs a bottle from the fridge, plunks into a chair, and stretches out his long legs.

"I had no medical training," Steve tells me, running his hand through his dark hair. "No anatomy, no histology, no oncology, none of that. My degrees were in marine biology and applied mathematics. But I knew enough about chemical processes that I was able to read textbooks and understand them. So that is what I did.

"Friendly doctors took me under their wing. I'd ask them what resources to use, and they would tell me: 'Read this book by that guy to understand this chemo-dynamic process.' So, I'd buy the book or get it from the library and read it."

After Janet's October surgery, Steve contacted other researchers at Mount Sinai, San Antonio, and Harvard about possible new drugs, and his own research went into high gear.

"I started talking with Chet Allard who was active in one of the adenoid cystic carcinoma or ACC groups," Steve says. "He worked on the research staff up at Harvard, and he and I became very, very, very good friends. The Harvard research team had come up with the idea of anti-angiogenic research and angiogenesis—using agents to starve tumors by denying them the ability to manipulate capillaries and grow a blood supply directed toward them. Chet was a past victim of ACC and came up with the idea of metronomic chemotherapy treatment. He used minimal doses of chemo like a metronome, very regularly, to constantly stress and dose the tumor, to keep it off base. In his case, it worked. But he liked my idea better.

"My idea, called Pharmacobiotics, suggested an anti-pathway agent to try to deny tumors the ability to form blood vessel supplies—using anti-angiogenic therapy not with chemicals but with a marker at a molecular level. Chet put me in touch with another researcher on the Harvard team who really liked my proposal. I already knew what Jan's markers were because they did an assay of her tumor before she went into the Prinomastat trial. I knew she was positive for matrix metalloproteinases, or MMPs, numbers 1, 2, and 9. I knew that. And I needed an agent that would suppress MMPs 1, 2, and 9, one that would close those pathways and starve the tumor."

I listen intently, trying to keep up.

"Their research suggested that doxycycline, which is literally cheaper than aspirin, was a broad-spectrum MMP inhibitor. So, I sent a sample of her tumor up to this guy. They slipped it into the assay testing with all the other patients' and didn't tell anybody. They since have been told they can't do that anymore, but they did it for us and confirmed that Jan's tumor was MMP 1, 2, and 9. If we could find an inhibitor, we could maybe stop them.

"So I talked to her primary care physician and said, 'Look, doxycycline can't hurt her and might save her.' The doctor said, 'Sure.'"

Janet jumps in. "At first, I thought it was so stupid," she says. "If my cancer is so serious, why would such a common, normal drug help me? They use it for acne! And my only restriction is that I can't drink alcohol because it interferes with the drug's effectiveness. No problem."

I try to wrap my mind around all Steve has just told me. He says he will get me a copy of Pharmacobiotics to read. Inwardly, I wonder if I'll have the energy to comprehend it. And me, a bio major.

"It's scary," Steve continues, "to think about what people do who don't conduct their own research. All the information we're working on and sharing among researchers and using to develop treatment plans will not likely reach the medical journals or the press for several years. I'm fortunate that my early papers on the web looking at inhibiting tumor pathways got attention and a group of top-flight researchers has kindly agreed to help me through these ideas."

"I thank God for all the people who have worked on me," Janet interjects. "Not to brag, but Steve always gets me the best doctors. He's been on websites, he knows the terminology, so he gets to the chairman. And they know he's not just some poor husband, but someone who understands, and they want to meet him. And they learn from him."

As the light fades, I thank Steve and Janet for sharing these memories. Janet walks with me to the door and we hug and hug again—the first hug, our joy that we got to visit again, the second hug, our promise to each other: We will meet again. I head into the early evening chill, get into my car, and turn on the heat. What an afternoon. My mind reels with the stories. Driving home, I question my fortitude to do the research Steve has done. To go through Janet's struggles. I can't imagine it. It's exhausting just to think about.

At home, I smile as *tea-kettle, tea-kettle, tea-kettle* reverberates from a Carolina wren in the holly. Every season, their vibrant songs ring through the woods in resonant voices far out of proportion to their tiny size. Severe cold can take its toll on their populations, but the survivors do not cower. They sing. Whether facing adversity or abundance, they sing.

44

Reading

Janet

JANUARY 2006

"Do you see any good ones?" Janet asks.

"Well, I'm not sure what you'd like. Let's keep looking."

We stomp around in Janet's basement, back in a storage area, looking at books.

"Ugh," Janet says. "Sorry this is such a mess. I've wanted to get down here and organize, but I haven't been able to."

"No worries! Who doesn't have spaces that need organizing? You should see my attic."

"Are you sure you don't mind reading to me?" Janet asks. "I dunno...it feels..."

"Like another loss?"

"Yeah. First it was eating, now seeing." Janet's shoulders slump. Earlier in our visit, she'd tried on every pair of glasses she owns. None offered a clear image.

"But you know what. I think this will be fun."

"Good. Here, what about this one?"

"Yeah, that'll do," Janet says, thumbing through the collection of stories by Washington Irving. She leads the way upstairs. The porch glass doors rattle. "Whew," she says, "Listen to that."

Fierce winds ahead of an approaching cold front spiral brown clusters of oak and maple leaves around the yard. The creek below kicks up in confusion, high tide waves colliding with the small dock. Nestling into the warmth of the family room under her blue knit blanket, Janet listens to the offered list of stories. "Rip Van Winkle," she chooses, and we spend the next half hour with Rip in the Catskills above the Hudson River, listening to ninepins.

"I just love the language he uses," Janet says, laughing at his turn of phrase, his wit. She settles into her blanket and closes her eye, her wistful crooked smile a sign of her serenity as the storm outside contrasts with Irving's words, the hush of the room, and the light of one lamp filling it.

The next afternoon, Janet sits on the couch, alone. Steve's at work, Steph at school. How slowly the hours go by. She's sick of television; every commercial seems to revolve around food. She dozes, rubs Woody's back with her foot, tries not to think, but once her mind starts up, frustrations and fears wheedle their way in. Every thought takes her to dread; she finds shutting down easier.

She gingerly touches the bandages on her face

where the four wounds remain open. All that radiation coming back to haunt me, she thinks, then gives a snort. But at least I am still here to haunt.

MRSA plus two other infections persist. Doctors at Beth Israel want to remove the titanium bracketry in her face to promote healing. Another big surgery: eight hours, another two-week recovery.

She rubs her ribcage and talks out loud, to herself, to Woody, after reading one of the doctor's emails. "How are they going to find enough tissue here to fix my cheek and my upper lip plus fill in my temple?"

I hate how my temple is dented in, she thinks. Surgeons say they can't fix my ability to swallow. How in the world am I supposed to get over ninety pounds when I can't swallow?

And they can't give me a prosthetic eye. Too much bone loss they say. Why didn't they say so in the first place rather than give me hope? The alternative— that patch that looks like an eye but doesn't move. No way. I look freaky enough. Doomed to be a Cyclops. I wish that sounded funny.

She picks up the whole pile of printed emails, and though she knows what they say, she holds up a magnifying glass to read them again. Results of the latest CAT scan: another lung tumor, three now, all growing. Results from ophthalmologists at the Wilmer Eye Institute at Johns Hopkins: cataract in right eye, the result of past radiation, is growing. But doctors won't operate until her vision worsens, and the MRSA infection has cleared. A copy of Steve's latest email he sends to family and friends reviews all this information but ends with: *The medical merry-go-round never seems to end. Right now, we are focused on getting weight on Jan, keeping her spirits up, and dressing wounds. Each is a full-time job. If there were ever a time for a miracle, it's now.*

She sets the papers on the table. Rests her head back and sighs. How many miracles am I allowed?

45

Regrets

Dotty

FEBRUARY 2006

Helen and I sit side-by-side on the couch, each on our own laptops, looking at her Myspace page. "Mom," she says, "I'll post Ruth's college acceptances here when she gets them in April. You can access my account and see where she gets in while you're in Egypt."

Egypt. Unbelievable. Traveling with Jonathan's parents and sister to this place I never imagined I would see. Even years from now, this magical trip will feel like a dream.

On Helen's page, I notice her answers to surveys: *Do you drink? Smoke? Do drugs?* Though pretty sure I could guess, I am relieved to see she has answered *No* to each question.

Do you get along with your parents? 75 percent of the time.

"Helen! Only 75 percent of the time?"

"But Mom! That's pretty good!"

We both laugh. I chalk it up to her need to look at least a little rebellious to her peers. Then I read the next question: *Do you have any regrets? Too many to count.*

"Too many regrets to count, Helen? I'm sorry, that must be a hard way to live." She does not respond.

At that moment, I couldn't think of any of my regrets, though suspected they were hiding. I've tried to live my life to minimize them—staying in touch with friends and family, traveling, spending as much time as possible outdoors. But now, a week later, regrets are crashing on top of me, my carefully concealed tower toppled by a teen.

The Susquehanna River glistens outside my window on the Southwest Airlines Boeing 737, flying north from Baltimore to Providence. The texture of the blue-brown water looks like the back of my hand, tiny creases holding the surface together. Is skin enough to hold me together?

One regret looms so large I have to keep taking deep breaths as it threatens to crush me: Why didn't we press doctors to take Mom more seriously. Her symptoms—shortness of breath, steady diarrhea— have been there for months. They'd gotten so bad that Patty pushed the issue, got her seen yesterday, and called me. I immediately booked a flight. Now lots of tests are happening, including a blood transfusion this morning because she is so anemic.

For the past few months, I've been calling ninety-year-old Mom every night at 5:00 to check in, making sure she was getting her supper ready—taking the meals Patty and I had prepared for her out of the freezer, putting them in the microwave, then onto the table. We'd chat to catch up on the day's events.

Yesterday, talking with Patty, and then Mom, we used the word. Cancer. The apprehension Patty and I have kept at bay for six years now roils inside us— the fear Mom's cancer would return. But Mom, ever practical, said, "Even if it is cancer, I'd rather know what it is."

After Mom was diagnosed with vulvar cancer in December 1999, she came down to Annapolis for Christmas to see our new house, then went home for surgery. "Why can't I have the kind of cancer you can talk about," she quipped when I went up to take care of her afterwards. "No one has any problem talking about breast cancer!"

Sometimes Patty and I wonder how much cancer we must endure. Our beloved grandparents, Mom's parents, each died of cancer, Grammy when we were fourteen years old and Grandpa when we were eighteen. Dad died nine years ago, having first survived bladder cancer, only to have aplastic anemia rob him of blood, his weekly infusions not enough to keep up with his bone marrow's decline. A horrible death. And I, three thousand miles away in White Salmon.

I had visited him and Mom often, tried to donate blood (ironically, too anemic, the nurse said to me every time), and played round after round of cribbage with him, one of our favorite games. We'd always raced each other on the newspaper's Jumble every night; he'd call out the letters from his chair in the living room while I did the dishes with Patty. A mathematician and machine designer by trade who'd gone to MIT night school, Dad published one book on a new and easier way to use the slide rule. But it came out just as calculators became popular and the books sat in an upstairs closet.

When we were six years old, Patty and I helped him solder the tiny transistors of the color television he was building from a Radio Shack kit. Our reward? At Smith Neck School, our school a mile down the road with two classrooms—one for first grade, one for second—where the bathroom lurked in the basement and the playground was a grassy field next to a giant pale blue water tower enclosed by a chain-link fence, we huddled with our first-grade classmates at recess and revealed a truth only we, the owners of the only color television of all our friends, knew: The Wicked Witch of the West was green.

He taught me chess when I was ten—on the wooden board he'd made and then veneered with intricate designs—but he also played by mail with another player. He would write down his move on a postcard in his precise all-capitals handwriting, mail it, then wait for his opponent's move inscribed on the postcard to arrive in the return mail. I can't imagine anyone now having that kind of patience.

When our girlfriends spent the night, we would

head to the game closet and get out the revolving wooden holder, each sleeve holding musty-smelling red, blue, and white poker chips. At the dining room table, Dad taught us the games: twenty-one; five-card draw, deuces wild, jacks-or-better-to-open; seven-card stud; night baseball; day baseball. We clung to hopes for a royal flush as we tossed in white chips for the ante, found the spunk to raise a blue when two pair burned in our hands, accepted reality when we got beaten by a straight.

These thoughts of home tumble through my mind as the plane ascends and levels out, the trees of southern Pennsylvania stark, leafless. Do I have the courage for what lies ahead? What I don't know yet is that after two pints of blood and a diagnosis of Crohn's disease, Mom will live another seven years and die a peaceful death in her living room with Patty and me by her side, holding her hands, at the age of ninety-six.

Looking now at the bare-limbed trees, toothpicks of lifeless brown, I find the idea of losing Mom gut-twisting; anguish I do not feel ready for, even at the age of 49. What must this feel like to Steph and Reid? What unspoken fears do they harbor late at night as they lie in bed? When they sit in a classroom while their Mom is in surgery, or home recovering but laden with infections?

Janet told me about losing her mom to cancer three years ago, about Doris's earlier cervical cancer—hidden from all except Lynn two decades before—which later returned as ovarian cancer. Two weeks before Doris died, Steve's dad died of liver cancer. Janet's dad died sixteen months later from prostate cancer that metastasized to his bones. Janet worries about Steph and Reid: What genetic legacy do they carry?

Like her mother did for her, Janet has tried to downplay her cancer to Steph and Reid, and for the most part, she has—until the surgery last fall. Now, her missing eye and contorted face cannot be missed, the open wounds and persistent infections an additional worry.

Yet, even now as the trees recede and we climb into the clouds, it's a fear of my own that rises, an old one punched to the head of the line yesterday. A fear I hardly dare name. It pushes Janet and Mom aside and swells in my core.

46

Heartache

Dotty

FEBRUARY 2006

"Water, please," I respond to the flight attendant, my mouth dry. Vivid memories swirl.

Summer, 1982. I was twenty-five, Jonathan was twenty-six. Married in June in a Quaker ceremony at Apponagansett Meeting House in my hometown of South Dartmouth, Massachusetts, we backpacked all summer throughout the west: the Rockies in Colorado, the Wind River Range in Wyoming, Glacier National Park peaks in Montana. We took macho pictures: glissading down snow chutes in boots-only attire, skinny-dipping in glacial ponds, hauling our huge backpacks over eight feet of July snow. We hiked to the top of the world, basked in sun-drenched meadows, hunkered down when fierce thunder-storms blew over us. We were young, strong, and in love. Nothing could stop us.

Autumn arrived and we returned to Maryland— I, to teach at Sandy Spring Friends School, Jonathan, to the endless and demoralizing task of looking for work in D.C., where a bachelor's degree plus several seasons as a National Park Service temp were proving inadequate. We lived in a dark roach-run apartment in Takoma Park, slept on a mattress on the floor of our undecorated bedroom. School consumed me as I taught all day, coached in the afternoon, returned home to a Jonathan-cooked dinner, then spent the evening grading and preparing for the next day. I was overwhelmed; he was flailing. For Thanksgiving, we decided to get away and visit our Earlham friend Elaine in Atlanta, in the home she shared with her husband and cat. Jonathan's allergies to cats had increased since he left home for college, so he used his new inhaler frequently to keep breathing.

Monday, I was back at work. An early snowfall found me coaching outdoor winter lacrosse with orange balls, easier to see in the white landscape. Decked out in layers of warm sweats and old fingerless ragg wool gloves, I was teaching beginners how to cradle when a breathless student ran up to me. "Your husband is on the phone and needs you right away." I sprinted the long driveway to the main office and grabbed the receiver lying on the desk.

"Jonathan?"

"I...I'm on the floor...and I can't move. I don't know what to do," the disembodied voice said. How could this be Jonathan?

"Okay, okay, I'm here, honey," I said, with more conviction than I felt.

"I don't know what to do. I feel so strange...What should I do?" he asked.

With embarrassing clarity, I realized I didn't know our address, though driving there was routine. We had moved in at the end of the summer and my mail came to school. I could not call for help.

"Okay, Jonathan. You need to hang up with me and dial 9-1-1. I'll wait here by the phone. Call me back as soon as you hang up with them." The room lost its edges and a black fog closed in as a feeling of utter powerlessness descended, cold fingers gripping my intestines. He was a half-hour drive away. How could I not know where we live?

A minute later, he called back. "They're on their way."

"What happened?" I wanted to know details, trying to make the unreal fathomable.

"I don't know. I was sitting at the dining room table making phone calls, and then I was on the floor. I don't know how long I was out. And it's hard to move. The phone fell off the table with me, so I called you."

"Oh, honey...okay, I'm here. Just keep talking." Sirens sounded in the background and I breathed a tiny, but inconsequential sigh of relief. The icy fingers kept their stranglehold on my insides.

"I think the paramedics are here...'Come on in. Yeah, well...I'm not sure.'" Then, I could hear their voices, Jonathan responding, but not their words. "Dotty? Just a minute," Jonathan said into the phone again. "One of the paramedics wants to talk to you."

"Hello? This is Jason. I'm an EMT. We're going to

take your husband in. He seems stable now. You can meet us at Washington Adventist."

I've never heard of this hospital.

Hurrying to my car after dismissing my athletes, with only a vague notion of the hospital's direction, I asked one of the coaches along the main drive on my way out. Fortunately, he knew where it was, and I drove, map in hand, suspended in the unknown, afraid to think too much. Traffic signals went by and I obeyed them, but only from habit; I was being pulled to Jonathan.

I burst into the emergency room and was met by a doctor.

"Do you know what ventricular fibrillation is?" he asked.

"Yes," I nodded, my own heart racing. In a rush of recall, my biology teacher's mind ticked off the detailed answer to his question: the heart's normal rhythm goes array, ventricles quiver, blood does not pump. Cardiac arrest.

"That's what just happened to Jonathan's heart. The EMTs were partially out the door with him when he went into V-fib and they had to get him back into the apartment and use the shock paddles on him. We don't know, but we suspect he'd already had a V-fib attack before they got there and somehow came out of it. Maybe when he fell out of the chair. You can see him now; we're getting ready to take him up to the Cardiac Care Unit. But be aware, he does have some burns on his chest from the paddles."

The doctor led me into a dark foreboding hallway. Lying on a gurney was Jonathan, pallid skin stretched over the bones of his face and chest; bandages covering the raw burns. How could a person look so pale? He smiled weakly, his eyes wide and terrified. Hugging him lightly around all the monitor wires, I squatted next to the gurney, my face level with his, and held his hand, repeating a mantra for us both.

"It's gonna be okay, honey, it's gonna be okay. We'll get this figured out; it's all gonna be okay."

Then they were taking him up to the CCU. I was told to meet them there in twenty minutes after they had him settled. He was wheeled into an elevator, leaving me in darkness.

At the well-lit main desk, the receptionist gave me directions to the restroom. I shut myself in a cubicle and wailed silently, gulping air. Desperate prayers swirled along with agonizing thoughts. How could this happen? He's so young—we were just backpacking! This isn't supposed to happen. What are we going to do? Please let him be okay, please let him be okay. I look ridiculous, I realized, looking down at my bright yellow sweats with their green SSFS and two crossed lacrosse sticks. I tried to stop crying but wasn't sure how.

In the ensuing two weeks, I spent every day with him, taking time off from school. Sitting with him first at Washington Adventist, then at Georgetown Hospital where he was transferred, I knew I had failed him. My standard response whenever he suggested something fun to do had been, I can't. Too much schoolwork to do. He was lonely; I was consumed. Though doctors thought the inhaler might have played a role, I was convinced my negligence, coupled with his sadness at not being able to find work, had led to his broken heart.

Two hospitals, twelve days, and no answers later, Jonathan was released. We had no extra money and no health insurance for him. Washington Adventist blessedly called us a charity case and dissolved our expenses. Georgetown allowed us to pay in tiny monthly increments—five to ten dollars—to each of the many doctors and services.

Just before Christmas, Jonathan and I returned home late one afternoon after a visit with friends, happy to be together as we walked up the steel gray stairway to our three-room second-floor apartment. We'd had no time to think about the holidays. We opened the door, and with only the light from the hallway penetrating the dark apartment, we gazed, stunned. There on our dining room table was a small fir tree covered in money—dozens of rolled bills tied on with red ribbons. Tears flowed as we contemplated who? how? Then we saw the little note card—from SSFS faculty and staff. These were not people with a lot of money, but they chose to share what they had with us, secretly, quietly, anonymously. We felt humbled and loved.

As the days went by, Jonathan and I never wanted to be parted. When we weren't in the same room, every sound put me on alert, wondering if he'd collapsed, ready to save him. He lived in constant fear. Panicky trips to the ER became part of our lives when his heart beat strangely. Every time, doctors sent us home with the same diagnosis—we don't know.

We felt safest together, so Jonathan gave up his quest for a job in natural resources in D.C. and came with me to school each day. First, he painted the inside walls of the meetinghouse, then was hired as a cook. The students, already used to freshly baked bread and good homemade food, delighted in his extra touches. We revolved around each other, my marriage taking on more meaning and importance. I strove for a better balance with Jonathan taking precedence over my job.

Knowing Jonathan needed a change and with the encouragement of his father, we moved to Philadelphia the following August: he to the University of Pennsylvania for graduate school in regional planning, I to teach and coach at another Quaker school, Friends Central. We moved into our duplex in Upper Darby, but dreaded the first Thanksgiving, especially the following Monday—the anniversary of his heart stopping. We made it through. A year passed, and another Thanksgiving loomed.

The whole month of November had become so difficult for us we could only breathe freely when we turned the calendar to December. I continued to monitor every sound as Jonathan moved about the house.

On the Monday after Thanksgiving we sat facing each other on our secondhand couch, apprehension breathing with us. We'd been doing the reevaluation counseling that Nancy Preuss from Sandy Spring had taught us, where pairs work together as co-counselors, taking turns listening while the other speaks of distresses in their life. I had been listening as Jonathan cried, verbalizing his fears. His heartbeat was feeling off—as it often did—and I was holding his hands. He said he needed a Kleenex and dashed up the stairs toward the bathroom. Then his body stopped, and he collapsed on the landing.

Racing to him, I called his name over and over, trying to shake him awake. Nothing. Needing him down the stairs to do CPR, I tried to lift him. How could he be so heavy? I dragged him to the floor, assessed his lack of pulse, and began CPR. The room closed in, the phone behind me seemingly hundreds of yards away. Only a dim light around us kept him close.

Suddenly he took a ragged breath and began yelling, clutching at me, his worst nightmares now real.

"No, no, no! Not again!"

He clung to me, terror raging through him. I stood and had him hold onto my shoulders as I reached for the phone on the wall to call for help.

"Is God with me?" he cried. "Am I going to be okay?"

"Yes," I assured him over and over. "God is with you...you're going to be okay." I needed those words as much as he did.

Some called it an "anniversary reaction," another V-fib attack exactly two years after the first, the body's plea for help. For the first week, I spent every minute with Jonathan the hospital allowed, returning home late at night to wait by the phone for someone on the UPenn Medical Center staff to call with words too unbearable to hear. I barely slept, could not eat without him. A food truck outside the hospital saved me. I bought one hoagie a day to eat while we visited, those sandwiches and his presence sustaining me.

During the second week, I returned to my students at Friends Central, driving home and jumping on the subway as soon as I could in the afternoon, even the afternoon when, while waiting in my car to exit the school, a school bus crashed into me, propelling my car into the middle of City Line Avenue, where miraculously I was not hit by oncoming traffic. At the hospital, Jonathan did Tai Chi, and I lay propped in his bed with ice brought by the nurses for my whiplashed neck.

Twelve more days with endless tests and doctor visits in the hospital. Still no understanding of what had happened but drugs this time that "might help." We were left with nothing to ground us, to help us believe this couldn't happen again. Except for one tiny omen.

The night Jonathan went into the hospital, a baby was born: Carrie, the beautiful daughter of our friends Jim and Pat. They lived only minutes away; we'd all gone to Earlham College; Jim and I both worked at

Friends Central. Carrie's birth at the same time as Jonathan's near death could not be a coincidence. For me, her first breath was a promise that Jonathan and I would get through this. Though medical answers were still on the horizon, this baby carried the message I needed.

At the time, cardiologists had recommended an internal defibrillator, which in 1984 meant open heart surgery, leads sewed onto the heart, and a four-inch box embedded in the abdomen. Jonathan refused such invasive treatment. We laid our hopes on the drug that doctors guessed might keep him alive.

Twenty-two years later, we're back in Maryland, and last week, Jonathan was diagnosed with osteo-penia—a side effect of the cardiac drug the UPenn physicians had prescribed. Our primary care doctor, Dr. Czapp, sent him to a new cardiologist, who said Jonathan seemed to have a disease similar to the newly understood Brugada's syndrome, also called sudden death syndrome. He was shocked that Jonathan had lived this long without an internal defibrillator and wanted to put one in right away. Technology had changed dramatically: much simpler surgery, the defibrillator a small disk the size of a pacemaker. We got this news yesterday, the day before I was to fly up to Mom's.

When Jonathan drove me to BWI airport this morning, he told me he certainly was aware of the pros of getting an internal defibrillator, but he couldn't help dwelling on the cons: It can feel like a horse kicking you in the chest; it might fire accidentally. Some people report a diminished quality of life, constantly anxious that it might go off. Jonathan worries that would be him. As he still worries about his heart. As do I.

Sitting next to him in the Honda's passenger seat, I wanted to yell, GET IT! He's been doing better; the drug seems to have helped and we can forget about it sometimes. But I see him check his pulse surreptitiously, hear him cough—a trick a cardiologist once told him could help re-establish a normal heartbeat. Jonathan knows how desperately I want him to have a defibrillator, but also that it's his choice. He has to live with it. Does he know, does he have any idea, how much I dread living without him? To me, a kick in the chest is an answered prayer.

Two weeks later, he got the implant. I named it My Little Friend.

The plane touches down in Providence, and suddenly, Jonathan feels very far away. The need to be with those I love, all at the same time, almost suffocates me. And my need for them all sets fire to my terror of losing them.

Where is the line between regret and forgiving myself? In this case, I realize it's impossible to be in two places at once. But too often these days, I find myself having to say, No, I'm sorry, I can't, and then struggle with the guilt of disappointing people.

When I admit my limitations, it honors who I am right now. It's so difficult to live with the continual regrets both of saying no, and of not being who I want to be. Frustration lives under my skin. It was so much easier and rewarding when I could say, Here, let me. I can do that.

As the plane taxis along the runway, I try to switch gears and anticipate seeing Mom. I will meet her at the doctor's office, hopefully, take her home, then later to any needed appointments, and not straight to the hospital. We will watch the Today Show over French toast, The Price is Right over grilled cheese, Ellen in the late afternoon, M*A*S*H with supper. I will cook quiches and her favorite lemon squares to freeze for later. We will gab as always, the topic never important.

My goal for this visit is simply to be present. Right now, she and Patty need me, and worries must be put aside about the places I cannot be, the people I cannot be with. Stress can be a causal factor in MS exacerbations and relapses; I must keep myself calm. Staying in good health is critical. So many people rely on me.

The plane arrives at the gate. Deep breath. Do what's possible. Don't leave believing you could have done more. Sounds like a noble plan, but I know regrets will follow me. It never feels like I can do enough. But I have to believe that what I manage to do—for Mom, for Patty, for Jonathan, for Janet—does make a difference.

Jonathan and Dotty, 2014

47

Sweet Oxygen

Janet

FEBRUARY 2006

Janet settles onto the thin mattress, surprised by its comfort. The pillows put by the technician beneath her head and knees ease her body. "Ready?" he asks.

"Ready!"

The slab slides her through a round blue door and into a tube just big enough for one. The door closes behind her.

I like that it's see-through, she thinks, and quiet. So much nicer than those MRI chambers.

Her whole body relaxes into the mattress. Her only job: breathe.

Intravenous antibiotics couldn't knock out Janet's triple infection of MRSA, pseudomonas, and E. coli; her wounds remained open, one with exposed bone. Her doctors at Beth Israel wanted her to come up for immediate surgery. Steve was not convinced; he felt they should wait.

In his search for answers to wound healing, Steve discovered hyperbaric oxygen therapy, a treatment often used for burn victims and diabetics. The New

York doctors balked, worried that pure oxygen would spur tumor growth. Steve judged otherwise, backed by his literature searches and a recent unpublished study conducted at the National Institutes of Health. He knew the processes of tumorigenesis and wound healing were different.

So, for two hours, four days a week, Janet reclines in the pressure chamber of 100 percent oxygen at the Baltimore Washington Medical Center. The plan: thirty treatments before her next reconstructive surgery and ten afterwards.

Janet knows the risk; her tumors could continue to grow. But she and Steve want to avoid another four months of open wounds after the next surgery. Six weeks of oxygen therapy now could put her in better shape for surgery—and onto a quicker path for healing.

Will this be the miracle they need? They hope so. They need so many.

48

Could You Pray with Us?

Dotty

MAY 2006

Birdsong surrounds us in Janet's backyard. I identify the red-winged blackbird's squeaks and *conk-la-ree* song; the cardinal's *pretty-pretty-pretty* and sharp chip note; the robin's tumultuous warble. Able to see only their movement and general size through the blur of her cataract, Janet is thrilled to learn their voices, and we spend long moments listening. Sweet serenity for us both.

We've barely seen each other this spring, fitting in only a couple of visits between her surgery and subsequent doctor visits, my travels to Massachusetts and Egypt.

"I have lots to tell you," she teases, "but I wanted you to read this first."

She hands me a copy of a three-page letter. "Steve read me a book earlier this year by Sister Briege McKenna called *Miracles Do Happen* and he wrote to her."

The letter was posted March 13, two weeks before her second reconstructive surgery:

> *Although I am sure you're terribly busy, I'm going out on a limb and sending this message to you in hopes of getting your attention much like Lazarus's friends got Jesus's attention when they lowered Lazarus through the roof.*

Steve tells her their story: about their daughter who confounded doctors and is now a healthy seventeen-year-old despite four open-heart surgeries; of Janet's survival and continual challenges, and about her pending reconstructive surgery.

> *This is where you and your book come in. We've always been torn between asking for Jan to be healed and finding the strength to endure what God has in store for us. However, we have been comforted by your guidance that we should not feel ashamed to ask for an outcome we desperately want. After 23 years of marriage, we are still eager for more time together and with our children.*
>
> *What you don't know is how innately good my wife is. Without ever trying to do so, she has touched the lives of many people, though, with her infirmities, she rarely travels. When I take her to the grocery store, she gets hugs from the clerks and pharmacists. Business at our parish office stops when*

223

I bring Jan around. Everyone sees her as an inspiration—overcoming physical obstacles and not losing her faith and optimism. However, each of us has a limit and Jan has reached hers. She always is thinking of and helping others—now she needs help. There is an army of people praying for her across the world. People from all faiths—Mormons, Protestants, Jews, Catholics—are praying for Jan's recovery.

We were hoping that you could pray with us. I'd say pray for strength and grace for Jan, but weak, human, and mortal as I am, I also want to pray for Jan's healing so we can have more time on this Earth together...

I apologize for the intrusion, but, like Lazarus's friends, we are desperate to get God's attention. We believe in the power of prayer. Could you pray with us?

My throat burns as tears threaten. I do quick math in my head. Married for twenty-three years, they've been battling Janet's cancer for the last seventeen.

"We haven't heard back from her," Janet says. "But it just feels good that maybe she read it, maybe she is praying for us."

She tells me about her last surgery. Eight hours. Doctors removed the metal bracketry in her cheek; moved skin, tissue, and muscle from her shoulder and rib cage to her face; closed all her wounds; repositioned her lip; filled in her temple depression.

"You should have seen my face. I looked like a puffed-up basketball!"

Today some swelling persists, but I see past it. Her scars, the shape of her face don't faze me. I only see her.

She tells me about more surgeries this summer to help continue the reconstruction, but then she interrupts herself.

"Oh! I have really good news."

"What?"

"You know how I did the oxygen therapy back in February. Well, the doctors figured out that the tumors didn't grow at all during those weeks. Steve thinks that maybe, just maybe, the doxycycline is working."

"You're a medical marvel," I say, giving her a hug. "Let's celebrate." I get a book from my bag, another short story. We've found it best to finish a story in one session. Too many interruptions to tackle a novel.

I read "The White Heron," Sarah Orne Jewett's story of a young girl who must choose between betraying the natural world she loves or helping the charming hunter who appears at her grandmother's woodland home. Steeped in Jewett's poetic voice, our minds wander with her through the deep Maine woods as we bask in Annapolis sunshine.

One month later, three days before her third reconstructive surgery, Janet and I begin Haven Kimmel's memoir, *A Girl Named Zippy*, each chapter its own short story. We'll be able to put it aside as needed without losing any plot line. And indeed, in two back-to-back visits, we get Zippy from birth to age seven before Janet returns to Beth Israel Hospital in New York.

Janet and I greet Zippy on every page: We race our bikes around the neighborhood with her, rescue a runty pig, dawdle in endless ways to avoid Sunday School. Her wildness feeds us; her sensibilities propel us to our own childhood experiences, commiserating with her as she jumps from ennui to elation, from exasperation to contentment. Zippy transforms the day's gray to glitter; Janet's every belly laugh, a blessing.

49

Pennies and Dimes

Janet

August 2006

Thank goodness I'm done, Janet thinks, lying in bed, back home in Annapolis the day after her fourth reconstructive surgery in New York. And I must say, I'm getting pretty good at this recovery stuff. Or maybe that's just the painkiller talking.

She spent one night in the hospital after this surgery before returning home. She'd needed four days after her third reconstructive surgery in June— one at the hospital, three at Lynn's. Since March, when the surgeons had to graft skin from other parts of her body, leaving her back and shoulder in significant pain, these last two surgeries have been like playing chess: removing this piece here, moving that one there, anticipating her body's next several moves. They've lengthened and straightened her left nostril with cartilage from her left ear, repositioned her lip, and removed some transplanted skin from her left cheek. But they couldn't do the vestibuloplasty to make more room between the inside of her left cheek and gum, and the depression in her temple remains.

She'd glanced in the bathroom mirror when she first got home. A bloody, swollen mess, she thought. Looks like I was beaten up instead of having surgery.

A penny on her bedside table turns her thoughts to her mom, how she misses her every day, gone now over three years. But Janet finds one consolation. At least she doesn't have to worry about me anymore. I know what it is like to worry about your child—whether she will survive—and it chews me up to think what I put Mom through.

Lynn and their mom sat by the phone for each of Janet's tests or scans, wondering what the news would be. Every time the phone rang, they jumped.

Janet clenches the penny in her fist. When Doris died, Lynn, Donna, and her husband Bob kept finding dimes—in Times Square on New Year's Eve, in all sorts of strange places, often when they were feeling sad. Janet kept finding pennies. They all felt it was their mom connecting with them.

Janet smiles when she thinks of the note she left Lynn after the June surgery. The night before returning to Annapolis, she'd been up wandering around after Lynn went to bed. Seeing a dish of change on the kitchen counter, she got a paper towel, folded it into a square, then added two dimes for eyes, a penny for a nose, and drew in eyebrows and a smile. Janet knew Lynn would get it.

50

The Dead Feeling

Dotty

SEPTEMBER 2006

I lie on my left side in bed, Jonathan curled against me, asleep. My depletion feels so absolute, I glance at my arms to make sure they are there. This morning, in desperation, I took a bristled brush and bleach cleanser to our tiled kitchen floor, trying to scrub away the grime of my frustration. I hate this floor. I hate being so tired all the time. I shouldn't be doing this. I have to do this. Scrub, rinse, scrub, rinse. Could a clean floor elevate me to a higher sense of well-being; a picked-up house release me from the bondage of myself; made beds and clean dishes offer internal peace and tranquility?

Inside, darkness reigns. When Jonathan hugs me, tells me he loves me, tells me his only purpose in life is to take care of me, I nod and tell him I love him too. Inside, his words drop into a deep inaccessible well. Any praise, kindnesses, or loving sentiments from anyone—I hear them, but cannot absorb them. The walls of the well are thick, the depth vast.

Tonight, though I could feel Jonathan's desire, I turned away, defeated, terrible guilt consuming me. I have nothing, I think. I am nothing. Metaphors arise for this feeling of depletion: cold mashed potatoes, tall grasses bent under a rushing stream, pencil shavings crushed on the floor, mud.

I listen to Jonathan's rhythmic breathing, remembering how, after his heart stopped—first time, second—I would lie awake for hours, listening to him breathe. Praying that this time we would be safe. His breath, now warm on my back, reminds me to be grateful. Tonight, he is safe. Me? I could turn to stone, drop through the bed, and disappear.

I wake too tired to move, my body like waterlogged wood left by the tide. For an hour, I lie motionless, thinking. No paddling today. Maybe a short walk in the park. Maybe not. Why must I continually wake exhausted after a full night's sleep?

Finally, hunger and the need to pee get me out of bed. I will myself to shower, dry my hair, dress. Downstairs, I must sit to rest. My heart pumps at a rate normal after exercise, not after putting on a T-shirt and shorts.

In these moments of extreme weariness, I grieve for my unfulfilled life plans: hike the whole Appalachian Trail, run a marathon, train for a triathlon. I did run a half-marathon once in my 20s...and tied for last. Even if my health had remained good, these life goals might not have been accomplished. Yet today, I look to these extremes with unusual longing.

Wishing to jump in the car with my backpack to hike in the mountains with Jonathan, instead, I try to make my breakfast without crying.

Eating my standard pancake breakfast, I long for the change of oatmeal, granola, scrambled eggs. But my irritable bowel seems to be getting more and more irritable as time goes by, shunning more foods. My two types of migraines have been linked to their own set of food triggers, and my herpes virus lurks, waiting for a nut or a seed to pass my lips so it can burst into a cold sore. My list of food limitations grows, seemingly monthly, and in years to come, will surpass what I can currently imagine. But with each regret over a variety of food I cannot eat, I think of Janet.

She misses food but does not dwell on it outwardly. With me, she instead giggles about hearing ginger ale bubbles in her ear, regales me on the deliciousness of certain smoothies she's discovered, swoons over fruit nectars. I take a leaf from her notebook and try never to bemoan what I cannot eat to others, but instead delight in what I can. I take another bite of pancake and savor the moment.

Energized from breakfast, I squat in our small garden to rip crabgrass, sedges, and the weed-from-hell-that-shall-not-be-named from our strawberry bed. These weeds have taunted me all summer. Grasp near their base to get the roots, pull gently to avoid dislodging any seeds until they're in the bucket, dump them in the brush pile in the woods. I should not be out here. But I am so tired of feeling tired.

Caught in my personal mélange of anger and deep frustration, combined with newly-learned-but-not-good-at-today self-compassion and understanding, I weed. I try to ignore the steel-gray cylindrical curtain descending into the core of my chest and abdomen. But I can feel it getting darker and tighter, trying to smother me. I call it The Dead Feeling. My thinking goes numb, my emotions teeter on the edge of tears. Normally dormant symptoms are showing their fangs: numbness in my left hand and arm; burning on the bottoms of my feet; buzzing in legs, arms, and along my upper back; stabbing pain in both thighs. I've named this last symptom STP—Stabbing Thigh Pain—because it feels as though little heated daggers are being thrust throughout my thighs at unexpected moments. Decision-making becomes difficult, even on the simplest things. All sound becomes noise; I want to hide in a quiet space. No music, no television. Reading is out; concentration is gone. And writing is out; too hard to think. I am not sleepy. Just gone.

I try to avoid this state. It hurts, both physically and emotionally. When the curtain descends, I must lie down. Must be alone. So I miss out on things: new adventures while traveling when compelled to stay in bed at the hotel for the day; conversation at a party when lured to the peace of a bathroom stall; birds to be seen, water to be paddled, woods to be explored when glued to the couch. Being social becomes difficult even with my family. Everything stops. Including my choice to "shake it off," "distract myself," or any other advice to "get past it." Fortunately, my family understands and does not say these things. They try hard, harder than I, to keep this depletion-state away. Jonathan is always encouraging me to sit down, relax. I tell him it's a good thing he goes to work, or I would never get anything done.

So, for these few minutes, here in the garden, I can do something. Feel momentarily productive; see progress. The need for something tangible is more critical than rest to keep my soul intact. It's the only way to tamp down my aggravation. I will get better at being gentle with myself. I am going to rest soon. But right now, I weed. This isn't meditative. It's survival.

51

I Am an Enigma

Dotty

SEPTEMBER 2006

After resting on the couch for two hours post-weeding, I drive to Janet's, my first visit since her fourth surgery. "Janet, you look beautiful," I tell her, and she brightens with a smile.

"I have something for you," she says. She bustles into her kitchen and rummages through the refrigerator, fussing that it needs to be cleaned out (whose doesn't), and hands me a heart-shaped cookie she brought back from New York.

Janet is always giving me gifts—cuttings from her Christmas cacti, a baseball cap from the Outer Banks, a paperweight of blue-swirled glass. When she can't get out herself, she instructs Lynn, who visits regularly, on what to find for me. Her generosity humbles me.

In the shade of her backyard, we stretch out on chaise longues by the creek. Janet's chair is layered with soft quilts to pad her bones. We face north, away from the afternoon sun, away from the glare that bothers her cataract-laced eye.

Across her cheek, a new band of skin gleams between bright red scars, but she looks vibrant in the sunshine, her freshly washed hair blowing softly. The large skin patch where her left eye used to be seems normal now; her eyebrow has been raised to where it belongs; the dent in her temple she worries so much about hardly shows.

Her nose has been fleshed out more, though one nostril does not work. Her mouth still does not open beyond half-an-inch, and then only on one side. Eighty-seven pounds. My own 140 pounds seem opulent to me, though at five-foot-eleven I am scrawny to my family. Janet tucks her legs under her. Emerging from her faded denim shorts, her thighs fold to her calves like a carpenter's ruler. Later, when we walk up the stairs, I marvel that she has the strength to walk.

I tell her of my August travels—to New England to visit family, then home for a week before driving north with Jonathan again, this time to Maine to take Ruth for her first year in college. In that month, besides surgery, more hyperbaric oxygen treatments, and a follow-up visit to New York, Janet's been seeing a gastroenterologist to try to figure out why she cannot gain weight, despite her 2000 calorie-a-day liquid diet.

Janet and I talk about my upcoming two-day fundraising walk for MS. My college buddy Elaine is flying in from Atlanta tomorrow. On Saturday and Sunday, along with her sister, we will walk twenty-one miles the first day, then ten miles the second, around the Annapolis-Baltimore area with hundreds of others. We have raised over $3,000 for the National MS Society.

Pangs of guilt mixed with sadness burble up. A year ago, when Janet wrote the letter to my Girl Scout co-leader and me before her October surgery when the surgeon removed her eye, she asked us a favor. She knew I had walked in numerous fund-raising walks and that the Girl Scout troop had hosted rest stops for the walkers.

> I have been wondering for sixteen years and finally, I am going to ask you what's been on my mind. Can the Girl Scouts ever do a walk-a-thon or something to enlighten people about how serious head and neck cancer is? Not much money goes into that research field because it is so rare. But now that I am in so many trials, studies, and hospitals, I realize how rampant it is. If something could be done, maybe Steph could play a large role in helping out. This might help alleviate all the worry and concern she has. It might be a fun scout project doing something no one else has done.

Although the girls were old enough to take the lead, I lacked the amount of energy needed to help organize and run a big event like that. I had to say no.

I rarely complain about my own physical constraints, especially to Janet—mine are so meager compared to hers. But this walk worries me. Elaine and I had joined two breast cancer three-day sixty-mile walks prior to my MS diagnosis in 2002. Training for those meant days of walking eight, ten, and fifteen miles. This time, my typical walks are one to two miles, occasionally three to five. How am I going to walk twenty? I rely on history. I recall my ability to walk fifty miles in the three-day MS Challenge with Elaine two years ago in 2004, easing my qualms that I would never be able to join the long walks again. But recent bouts of weariness concern me.

Today, four days after the walk, I slap my knee regaling Janet about my weekend.

"Janet, you should have seen me. I don't know where my energy came from, but on the second morning, I was bouncing down the streets of Baltimore in sandals. And that's after walking the whole twenty-one miles the day before. Check out my toe."

My big toe—the nail two shades of purple from bleeding underneath. Sneakers had to be abandoned, the nail too excruciating to touch.

Fun rest stops had kept us moving: people dressed as pirates commanding us to *Walk the plank* across a board laid on the sidewalk; a Hawaiian-themed stop serving us spirit-boosting slushies and decorating us with parrot stickers as we played a shell game to win a rubber ducky. "Janet, we had a blast."

I am an enigma. Even to myself. This is what I say to Jonathan when he shakes his head in wonderment when I tramp up a mountain, rake the leaves in our yard, or shovel the snow off the driveway with giddy enthusiasm. Some days, or parts of days, are like that. But they don't last. And I pay for my gusto.

Janet lets me be as I am during our visits. She doesn't question my range of energy from hilltop to wagon rut but accepts me as is. Her genuine under-standing helps normalize me and allows me to feel that my fluctuations are simply different feelings and abilities at different times on different days. My fuel level rests between a quarter tank and empty; its rise and fall fickle, erratic.

Home from Janet's, exhaustion consumes me. It's been a long week. Not only did I walk every step of those thirty-one miles, but I also took notes the entire way, adding the experience to my feature story for the *Bay Weekly* about fund-raising walks. Shuttling our daughters, running errands, plus getting ready for another flight up to Massachusetts tomorrow also chipped away at my energy. Monthly weeklong trips up to Mom's have become routine ever since she was sick in February. It gives Patty, who lives nearby and visits her every day, a break.

Wiping away tears of depletion, I flop onto the couch. And do nothing. Absolutely. Nothing.

52

Restoration

Janet

From her lounge chair in the backyard, Janet watches Steve and Reid tinker with an engine. They are both into the buy-'em-and-fix-'em-up routine because they appreciate fine cars but can't afford them. Relishing the challenge, they buy used or damaged cars and get them working again.

Reid has followed his Dad around since childhood. Quick to pick up each skill, he's retracing Steve's footsteps, who learned car repair from his grandfather but surpassed him at age thirteen. After years of fiddling and mending, Steve can restore anything. If he wants a boat, he builds it. His expertise has served him and them all well. Scrimp has become their byword.

Janet and Steve started out, as Steve liked to say, dirt poor. They'd both had to pay for their own college educations, then started in low-paying jobs, so they knew how to save. But these last years, with all their out-of-pocket costs for her surgeries' co-pays plus travel and housing for treatments in Seattle and San

Antonio, they couldn't afford new cars, or to replace things when they broke. Steve fixed them.

His repaired cars and designed boats were fun to own but also served, at times, as needed funds. Steve sold his favorite Pontiac GTO and a mahogany runabout to pay for the trip to Seattle for Janet's first radiation.

If insurance hadn't covered the experimental treatments in Seattle and San Antonio, they probably would have lost their house. But the heads of the radiology departments at the two universities called the insurance case reviewers to argue for them. Saying *I run this place and tell you, she needs this* made all the difference.

Steve and Reid chatter; grackles gather and bluster in the trees; a downy woodpecker whinnies his cascading song. Two chickadees fuss in the Rose of Sharon.

But Janet hears none of it. All she can hear is her own grating voice tumbling through her head. Her prayers feel like band-aids, not antidotes, to the constant depressing poison. The band-aids get drenched and fall away.

I will never go back to church, she thinks. Why do people have to stare? Why? Even after Steve leans forward and says, "Didn't your mom tell you it's not polite to stare at someone who's different from you?" He said that to a 50-year-old man! Oh, some people there are so nice, but I just can't take the others. Sorry God, we'll have to talk here. I just can't go back.

And God, why can't I see? I am down to one eye. Is it too much to want to see out of it? Or to eat? If I can't see, why can't I eat? Couldn't I have just one back? Just one? I know I should be grateful for what I have, and I am, but... A sob shudders through her. Her shoulders shake, and she bends forward, her arms crossed strait-jacket-style around her chest.

"Mom?" Reid asks, coming over and putting his hand on her shoulder. "Are you all right? What's wrong?"

"Nothing, Reid, it's nothing. I'm okay. Really. I'm fine, I'm fine. Go back to the engine." She shoos him away with a wave of her hand and a small smile.

She's not okay, and she knows it. But what else can she say to her son? It's the same old story, the one her family knows so well—but she's living inside it, and with the sadness that bubbles up when she least expects it, becoming volcanic, hot and overflowing.

I try so hard, God, not to let anyone see. At least there are no tears—ha!—that huge dose of radiation in Seattle zapped those ducts long ago...but oh, how I wish I could eat. Something, anything! I am so tired of Boost, of ginger ale—even smoothies, though those Gorilla ones from Robeks are good. I miss food. Every event—birthdays, Easter, Thanksgiving—food. Three times a day—food. I am surrounded, yet can't dig in. Like those people in life rafts after their ship sinks, surrounded by saltwater, but can't drink. Well— I guess they could drink, but then they would die. And I am alive. Alive, yes, but this sadness is killing me. God, are you even there? Are you listening? Do you even care?

"Mom? Are you okay? What can I do?"

"Nothing, Reid, don't worry." Janet shakes her head. "Thank you, I'm fine."

Three days later, Janet walks out to get the mail. Probably just bills and junk, but at least it's an excuse to get out of the house. She finds a dozen envelopes all addressed to her, but doesn't recognize the return addresses. Gathering them up, she rushes inside.

The cards come from all over the country. Some religious, some flowery, some funny—*I heard you were feeling droopy and poopy*, accompanied by a picture of a hound dog.

Cards keep arriving all week. She learns later that Nancy, a co-worker of Steve's, is part of an organization called Vanda's List. They do fundraisers, then use the money to buy and send cards to people who are sick.

Their messages stun her. All these people saying, *I've heard about your long battle with cancer and I want you to know I am thinking about you and praying for you.*

"Well, God," Janet whispers. "I guess maybe You have been listening. Maybe You haven't forgotten me after all."

53

Compass Needles

Dotty

November 2006

Ash-gray water ripples against the hull of my kayak. Through the haze of fog, I identify birds by silhouette: large dark geese, low-slung loons, erect tails of hundreds of ruddy ducks, round charm of buffleheads. Then, glowing through the gauzy air, the unmistakable ivory of the tundra swans, newly arrived migrants, back from northern breeding grounds.

All at once, fifty swans run, their black fleet slapping the water as they power into flight. Their high alto voices ripple across the morning, their wings singing with every pump of massive breast muscle. Long necks outstretched—yearning, seeking—they fly forward into the dim light and fade. White feathers glitter for a moment in the distance as they bank toward shore, then blink off, then on, then gone.

What a distance these swans, family groups including five-month-old cygnets, have traveled from

Alaska's ponds and stubby growth to this saltwater bay surrounded by great gray trees whose yellow leaves are beginning to drop. Every fall, 4000 miles here; every spring, 4000 miles back to the North Slope of Alaska on the Beaufort Sea.

They fly with purpose. They've been flying for weeks; it's in their very being.

At meeting for worship last Sunday, I sat in the usual silence, and again that image of a thick straight black line showed up with its jagged up-downs off to the left. Then, in what still feels miraculous to me, a fountain pen appeared at the end of the jagged line. Had those black lines been ink all along? I've been writing feature stories for the *Bay Weekly* all summer. Could this truly be my new direction? With breaths of elation and release, I recognized I had become a writer.

But Janet's compass needle was not so true. It fluttered with every breeze.

I sit with Janet on her back porch. A rare November day, 70 degrees. Janet is wearing shorts.

"Steve wants to go to Cape Hatteras. I don't know. I told him to go without me. I mean what can I do? He said, 'No way.'

"I thought yesterday was Friday, and I got up and showered and vacuumed. I thought you were coming over. Then I realized it was Thursday. It was a bad day."

A week later, the weather turns cool. Janet wears soft pink socks, jeans, a fleece jacket.

"I was always about 112–117 pounds," she says. "I had all the nicknames—Skinny-Minny, Bones— but they didn't bother me. The only nickname I really didn't like was one my dad called me. Puny Head. That made me so mad!"

I mention my childhood nicknames—Jolly Green Giant, Moose—and she insists on knowing the story behind each. Jolly Green Giant was simply because I was so tall—my friends' heads barely reached my shoulder until high school when they all began to grow. Moose came after a high school basketball game, the first one we varsity girls were allowed to play at night in the "boys" gym—the new full-size gym with bright lights and bleachers. We'd played just before the boys' game, both varsities going up against our rival New Bedford's teams, known for their height and aggressive play. My team won that night, and afterwards, as I relaxed with teammates on the bottom bleacher waiting for the next game, a young boy, about nine years old, approached me. "Was you da big moose that just stomped on dat otha team?" My friends, sporting the nicknames Teddy and Rubberduck, fell to the floor in laughter, and my nickname, Moose, was born.

Where I was tall, Janet was thin. And getting thinner. Cases of high-protein Boost sit in her front living room. She drinks several cans a day trying to get her weight up.

"I made it to eighty-eight pounds," she says, "then one day to ninety."

We chat about being moms—about having to let our eighteen-and-nineteen-year-olds find their own ways, even when it means leaving us. I try to normalize life for her, to let her know her kids are simply being kids, as mine are; teens trying to navigate their way. I feel like her touchstone with reality. She worries her children don't want to be around her because of her face.

"Reid came home yesterday, and I hid because I thought his girlfriend was coming in," says Janet, "but she stayed in the car. I asked Reid to help me make my bed, but he said he couldn't stay. He blocks me out. I think he doesn't want to accept what is happening to me."

Reid is a lovely young man, busy with his degree in engineering and his social life. He's at the age when most children leave home. But Janet, caught in her own web of vulnerability, feels abandoned.

"Janet," I say, "it's natural for them to want to be off with their friends, to sequester themselves away in their rooms with their computers. Mine do the same thing."

She looks at me, awed. "Really? Ruth and Helen are like that, too?"

"It's their age. They are supposed to break away from us."

But I know she is in a different place than I am. While I have the luxury of looking forward to visits and holidays, to the possibilities of marriages and grandchildren, Janet knows her future with her children holds no such promises.

Beside her vulnerability, however, lies mettle. On one of my recent visits, Reid came by with a friend who greeted me and in the next breath asked about my MS. I answered, but noticed Janet frowning, growing tense. When Reid and she left, Janet bristled.

"How dare she ask you about your MS," Janet grumbled. "Your health is your own business and she shouldn't have said that." I stopped her.

"It's okay, Janet. She was one of my Girl Scouts a couple of years ago. And I've written about my MS in the *Bay Weekly*. I don't blab about it, but it isn't a secret."

"Well," Janet said. "I think it's rude that she asked."

Janet's fierce loyalty to her kids and whole family is indisputable, but I hadn't seen her protectiveness bestowed on me. She was furious. I was touched.

She takes a sip of water from her squirt bottle. Our conversation moves to disability insurance, and how she has been denied Social Security disability. After working for nineteen years, she quit her IRS job the day before Reid was born. Any chance to return to work was quashed by cancer.

"Look at me," she says. "I certainly look disabled." She wraps her fleece blanket tighter around her legs, tucks them under her, rests her head on the couch.

I tell her about my denied disability by a private insurance company through work, and how it took a lawyer to finally win. I didn't have MS, they said. Too healthy, they said, despite neurological evidence to the contrary.

"They just didn't get it," I tell her. She shakes her head. We sit in silence.

Nine years from now, on a warm summer evening, I will throw my cell phone across the room after reading an email from my lawyer. The company not only will have canceled my disability insurance but will have stalked me as well: parked outside my house for two days; followed me on a mile drive to the beach to see if the swans had arrived; followed me on a walk in the park next door, hiding while I photographed an owl. Even my five-page rebuttal trying to make them understand the vagaries of MS fatigue, plus my doctor's evidence and my lawyer's fight, won't restore the payments. *You shook out a rug,* they'll write. *You wheeled in a recycling bin.* Two years later, the lawyer will convince them to settle out of court. I'll receive less than a third of what they owe me.

Janet loads pink liquid hydrocodone into a syringe, shoots it into her mouth, and swallows.

"My face hurts all the time," she tells me. "Plus, my sinuses feel like there is something inside them. They hurt and itch, so I use a little paintbrush and rub the outside skin." She says this matter-of-factly, stating what is.

She brushes above her right eye, across her forehead. Neither of us wants to say what we are thinking. She tells me the doctors say the odd sensation is a result of the radiation. We both try to believe that.

I lean over and give her a hug.

"Do you have time for more *Zippy*?" she asks.

"Always."

I read the next chapter of Kimmel's book, falling again into her easy humor. My heart soars as Janet giggles, exclaiming over the zany stories, like Zippy's mother convincing her she was bought from gypsies. The overcast afternoon slips along. Woody sleeps at our feet. Yellow leaves trickle onto the grass.

She tells me her cataract surgery will be in January.

"It makes me nervous," she says, "but I can't see now, so I guess it's worth a try. The doctor is convinced it will work."

She ponders aloud about the tumors in her lungs, the one at the base of her skull: "I think about them, wonder if they're growing. They'll get me someday," she says. "But not yet."

54

The Hawk

Dotty

MARCH 2007

On this early spring day, I relish every woodland song catapulting from the throats of the cardinal, wren, and towhee. An eastern phoebe flits off a branch, snags an insect, and flits back. The arrival of spring migrants helps ease my sadness over the annual departure of the tundra swans. Yesterday, the first osprey flew overhead. Today, chipping sparrows trill in the fields; magnolias bud into fuchsia lipsticks; tiny maple seeds blush.

Then a ruckus starts up. Crows and blue jays scream; titmouses and chickadees chatter and bluster. Charging toward the hullabaloo, I hope for the great horned owl.

Searching high in the still-bare branches, amongst the mélange of fuss and squabble, I finally see the focus of their agitation. A red-shouldered hawk sits on an exposed branch. Haughty, noble.

Every little bird is on the alert, doing everything in their power to chase away this threat. But the hawk, unperturbed, glances out over the canopy and stays put.

Janet's cataract surgery two months ago went off without a hitch, but today I watch as she assembles old glasses on the coffee table and tries on each pair. Several years from now, I will do the same kind of searching, except my assortment will be shoes. I will try pair after pair—my sneakers, crocs, sandals, hiking boots—trying to find something to ease the neuropathic pain in the balls of my feet, which feels like hard clumps of burning clay. None of my shoes will work.

"I'm just worried my sight's not going to get better," she says.

Finally, she gives up. Glasses cannot correct her blurry vision. At least not yet.

She shows me the results of her latest CT scan from Johns Hopkins. The tumor at the base of her skull has remained stable; the three lung tumors have grown, but minimally. "Maybe," she says, quoting a Steve email, "our custom-designed clinical trial of one is still working."

With Janet's tumors calmed, I try to subdue my trepidation of losing her. The latest surgeries—to reconstruct her face, to fix her cataract—have focused not on keeping her alive but on improving her quality of life. I try not to judge their merit, whether they were needed or not. If she and Steve and the doctors agree they are necessary, that is enough for me. But for all the surgeons' work over this past year, the results have not measured up to expectation. Janet is still unhappy about her looks; she still cannot eat.

Steve and Janet are cautiously thrilled that the doxycycline seems to be doing its job. They do not know that Steve's efforts will be sabotaged by the most unlikely person.

Janet and I talk about the future as though she still has years to live. We try to believe it. Steve does too. But we know that all the repairs, the fixing, and the contouring are not a cure. The hawk remains.

55

What
Sustains Us

Dotty

I wake, and eyes still closed, do a quick assessment. Feel okay, just tired. Saturday morning. Jonathan's probably already been to the farmers market, done the shopping. I hope he remembered to get eggs. I'm sure Helen's still asleep. Ruth's at Colby. I open my eyes, look at the clock. 8 a.m. Good. I slept in.

I turn over, and there, lying next to me, is a cantaloupe.

"Jonathan! Get this thing out of here!" I hear him laughing. He knows the smell of cantaloupes repulses me. I can't stand the loathsome things in the house, make him seal them in plastic wrap when they are in the refrigerator, and would never eat one, much less cuddle with one in bed.

"What's the problem?" he asks, smirking as he comes through the door. I point, shrieking.

"Get it out of here!"

"Okay, but just think, now when you come downstairs for pancakes, there will be a delicious smell when I slice it open and eat it with lime and honey. Doesn't that sound good?"

"Aaaargh! No! Get it out of here. If there weren't screens in the window, I would launch it myself."

Jonathan's teasing is legendary. Back in his White Salmon office, when rubber snakes spilled from a jammed copier, when a motion-sensor rubber rat squealed and writhed in the lawyer's desk drawer, when a cardboard full-size image of the Bartles and Jaymes guys waved from the roof of the office building the morning we moved away, his office mates knew who to indict. And who to get back at. Such wonderful camaraderie helped ease the daily work amidst contentious factions—land and homeowners on the one side, environmentalists on the other, and the Gorge Commission in the middle, trying to maintain the scenic view of the Columbia River.

Laughter buoys us all. Mom and I can be reduced to tears, unable to speak, over something silly we thought of or saw on television. An episode involving the legendary antics of Dick Van Dyke when he spotted a snake had us howling and crying at the dining room table. Goofing around with Jonathan and the girls can get me laughing so hard I fall to the floor. Patty and I can set each other off with a single word. Such grand release. It is what sustains us.

"Dotty! I can't believe I am paddling my own boat!" Janet laughs as she pats the blue wooden hull on its inaugural voyage. "But, boy, am I out of practice."

"You're doing fine," I say, paddling right behind her. "Remember, we don't have to go far."

Last year, Steve and Reid built Janet a one-person kayak after surgeons used muscle from her shoulder to help contour her face. The paddling, they hoped, would be good physical therapy to get her shoulder back in shape. Today, she finally has the energy to give it a try.

"Let's head down the creek to the bend," Janet chirps, but she has trouble making headway as her boat drifts toward one shore then the other.

"This is a lot of work," Janet giggles as she paddles back and forth. We finally make it to the far side of the creek, then stop in the shade to rest. "I just can't believe it," she says again. "This is so much fun. Okay, I'm ready, let's go."

We set off, but a hefty breeze thwarts her efforts and soon the struggle tires her. "I think I better go back, Dotty. Sorry to make this so short." But she can't get turned around.

"No worries," I say, jumping out of my kayak and grabbing Janet's bow line. I haul both boats back toward their dock, feeling a mix of exhaustion-onset and exhilaration as I squelch along in the muddy channel, the water shoulder-deep.

"I feel so useless," Janet says, frowning, her shoulders slumped.

"Nonsense. It was just too windy today. We'll try again next week."

"Yeah, definitely," Janet replies, flashing her crooked smile.

We never go out again.

56

Party

Dotty

With the help of her sisters, Janet pulls off a surprise party for Steve's fiftieth birthday. She's been filling me in on the plans during our visits—the food, the decorations, and the guest list: family, friends, and all of Steve's coworkers.

What an enormous success! I watch as Janet runs up and down the steps from kitchen to patio, sits for a moment to chat with a friend then heads off to refill the chips, get someone a beer.

But for this day, her concerns about herself are tucked away; her energy is boundless. I marvel at her, unsure whether to laugh or cry.

57

Surgery Number 5

Dotty

DECEMBER 2007

On a trip through Germany with Jonathan's family, I have Janet on my mind. In Bamberg, we enter the Dom, a thirteenth-century cathedral. I check the time, 1:30 p.m., 7:30 a.m. in Baltimore. Time for Janet's surgery. I light a candle at the front of the stone church.

For the past few months, Steve has persisted in researching the best surgical team to continue Janet's reconstruction. Though familiar with the surgeons at Beth Israel in New York, Steve and Janet found an innovative team in Baltimore at Johns Hopkins. With a bit of trepidation, but greater hope, they've chosen Johns Hopkins for Janet's fifth facial reconstruction.

"For you, Janet," I whisper. I watch the flames. So many candles. So many lives. I pray for yours.

58

Still Here

Janet

MARCH 2008

Janet rubs her forehead, around her eye, wishing vaguely that her touch alone could banish the pain that lingers, could dissolve the hard bumps. Wonders if scarring is the reason her sinuses can't drain.

"I do wonder sometimes what's under there, Dotty," she says as we sit on our couches. She doesn't try to answer her own question, doesn't want to go where her imagination leads.

In December, the Baltimore surgeons accomplished most of their goals for Janet's face and mouth. But they were reluctant to take on the swelling in her lower right eyelid, unsure of its cause. Something to watch, they said.

"I saw the surgeon again," she says. "He's not going to do any more internal surgery. He may get rid of the fat in my cheek, try to fix my nose and maybe my eye. My local ENT doctor will do my eustachian tube. I'm glad they won't do any more internal work."

Two and a half years of surgeries. None has made a difference in her ability to eat—still a liquid-only diet—and she can barely see. Whenever others tell her she looks good, she withers inside and feels sadness enshroud her. It isn't good, and you know it, she wants to tell them. But to herself, she acknowledges that this face is as good as it's going to get.

Janet muses over her years with cancer.

"The hardest part about being in cancer wards," she says, "is seeing everyone dying from it.

"I went for a follow-up after surgery a couple of months ago. There were three of us in the elevator, Steve, me, and another woman. She looked at me and said, 'Were you the lady in the bus crash?' And I said, 'No, I just had surgery. Why? Were you there when the crash happened?' And she started to laugh. 'Oh no...I just thought...I mean...your face...I figured you'd been in the accident.'

"And she kept laughing. She thought she was so funny. Steve just put his arms around me and turned me away from her. He really wanted to say something to her but said nothing."

She sips more water from her squirt bottle.

"My nose keeps getting more solidified," she says, pushing at it. "I don't want any more surgeries because I don't know how it will heal. People who have been blown up by grenades have gotten new noses, but reconstructing someone's missing nose is easier than dealing with mine that's gotten so hard. When they try to get rid of the scarring, I worry they will do more damage.

"Nineteen years ago, I would not have bet anything I would be alive today. The doctor gave me six months to live. Then there was that pregnant doctor at Hopkins who told me there was no hope. To just give up. Steve kept saying, 'She's wrong, she's wrong.' It took me a year to get over her saying that. Actually, it still bothers me."

The wound that never healed.

Then she giggles.

"At different times, in different hospitals, doctors who'd worked on me ages ago would see me and say, 'Oh my gosh! Janet, you're still alive!'

"Yes," I'd tell them. "I am still here."

59

Favorite Saint

Dotty

April 2008

Janet has already laid cushions on our lawn chairs and set out a water bottle for me. We nestle in her backyard, soaking up the day's warmth after several days of rain. Another storm front arrives tomorrow.

"I'm so tired today," Janet says. "Maybe because the weather is strange. I'm always so tired at the end of the day. But I pull out a chair and Steve scratches my head and that is very comforting."

We are both oh-so-tired.

This morning, though too exhausted to make my breakfast, I knew I would not cancel my afternoon visit with Janet.

Having a friend like Janet puts life into perspective. When my self-pity looms, I think of the vastness of all she deals with. But belittling my symptoms compared to Janet's out loud to my family prompts them to remind me it's not a contest. We each struggle in our own way.

Janet, with all she's been through and faces every day, still feels compassion for others. She talks about friends with cancers or diseases, about the concern she feels for them, wondering how best to help. Her greatest sorrow is for a friend whose teenage daughter, a twin, has terminal cancer.

"I am so sad for her," Janet says. "They only give her a few months to live, but they are going to do chemo to try to slow it down. Her twin sister is going to shave her head too. I sent a card, but just wish there was more I could do.

"Only seventeen. I was lucky, got to have my teenage years, my twenties, travel, and work. Even though I couldn't raise my kids the way I wanted to, at least I got to try."

A mixed flock of birds descends, and the singing pulls our attention toward the trees.

"What's that one?" Janet asks.

"Red-bellied woodpecker," I tell her, describing the sound.

"I know peter-peter-peter," she says, laughing. "Titmouse!"

Birdsong tutoring continues as we listen to chickadees, a white-breasted nuthatch, the ever-present red-winged blackbirds down in the marsh. Ease settles into me; the weight of exhaustion lifts.

Comfortable with silence, we bask in song and sun. We've missed each other these last two weeks while Jonathan and I traveled to Tucson, Arizona. I promised to return with stories.

I describe the many species of hummingbird and oriole, and my favorite desert sounds: the whirring songs of the cactus wren and canyon wren. Recall the hilarity of my nonstop sneezing while prowling through blooming desert scrub in search of elusive songbirds; our joy when we spotted a rare red and green bird, the elegant trogon, in the mountains; our thrill heightened when we heard the sudden warning of a baby rattlesnake inches from my boot.

Reaching into my backpack, I hand her a gift: a candle from San Xavier del Bac, an eighteenth-century Catholic mission south of Tucson. Painted on the glass is St. Jude, the patron saint of lost causes.

Janet nods, her eye twinkling. "He has been my favorite saint for a long time."

PART 3

we part

59

Scan Angst

Dotty

APRIL 2008

Mayapple shoots have shoved their way through the thick duff of soggy oak leaves and opened into small woodland umbrellas. Previous walks in the woods behind Sandy Spring Friends School linger in memory; pink-veined spring beauties festooning the understory dabbled with trout lily and rue-anemone. Our park next door, mostly secondary growth from an old farm, holds none of these lovelies, so I hold on to the wildflowers that do appear: the mayapple, violet, Jack-in-the-pulpit, crane fly orchid. I hold on to what I can.

Standing at the sink, washing the supper dishes, I hear the phone ring.

"I wanted to let you know that Janet can't meet with you tomorrow as you'd planned," Steve says. "Janet wanted to call herself, but her tongue feels so thick she can't talk.

"We had a bit of a shock to the system this week. Janet's post-op appointment after her eustachian tube surgery went fine, but routine test results showed a potential problem.

"We found out that a tissue sample from her nose tested positive for cancer. This is the first time in the history of her cancer that it has crossed the midline of her face from left to right."

My arms and torso shiver.

"She's having an emergency battery of tests this week, four CT scans and a CT-PET scan, to see if this is just a random set of cells or something more. Janet's visibly nervous, plus now we go through scan-angst. We jump every time the phone rings."

61

Are You There?

Janet

APRIL 2008

Why did Reid do it, Janet muses, lying in bed after Steve has left for work. To hurt me? Scare me? I don't know. But I do know I hate that motorcycle. And I'm not too keen on his girlfriend either. Or his housemates.

And what about Steph. She keeps trying different courses, different directions at the community college. I hope she can find her way. She has so much potential.

Janet can't help it—she worries. About her children, Lynn's upcoming flight, the girl with terminal cancer. Her personal cauldron bubbles: How long do I have, how will this end, what's coming next.

I wonder if I am losing my faith, she thinks. But if I say Goddamn it, I guess I still believe there's a God. Sometimes, I think He has forgotten me. But I guess not.

62

Happy Birthday to You

Dotty

APRIL 2008

I hold the bottles of nectar—apricot, peach, and pear—in the cake pan as Helen winds purple ribbon around them, makes a bow, cuts off the ends at an angle. Using bits of clay as glue, we stick small pink candles onto the lids along with tiny dried-orange flowers on toothpicks.

We drive to Janet's house. Steph answers the door and whispers hi. We tiptoe into the darkened family room where Janet, groggy from a nap, raises her head from Steve's lap.

"Happy birthday to you, happy birthday to you," we sing quietly. Janet smiles.

"We brought you a birthday cake," I tell her, kissing her forehead.

"Thank you," she rasps.

We don't linger, so she can sleep. Now she has a cake for her birthday. She can blow out the candles and make a wish.

Good news arrives the next day.

Steve calls. "The CT scans show no new growth in the tumor at the base of her skull and only minor growth in the lung tumors. As to her nose cancer, well, no one had ever checked it before, so maybe it's been there all along. If it doesn't change, then there's no problem.

"I like calling people with this kind of news," he says.

63

Teeth

Janet

MAY 2008

Janet hustles to the front door wearing her favorite silky red pajamas and fluffy pink robe.

"Hi, Dotty," she says, her voice hoarse as she reaches her arms out for a hug. We look into each other's eyes, laugh, and hug again—a so-happy-we-can-still-be-together hug, a blessing on this blue-sky day.

"I hope you can understand me today," she rasps. "My tongue is so tight. First, I can't eat, now, I can't talk. Everyone's happy about that but me!"

Settling onto her couch, she tells me about an upcoming conference on salivary gland cancer, with a panel studying better ways to address that form of cancer. She hopes what she and Steve have discovered will be discussed.

"If I ever need more cancer treatments, I hope it won't be in a clinical trial, like the Prinomastat trial, because what if I get the placebo? And they always make me sign privacy statements. Does that mean the results won't be public? I want people to learn from what I have gone through. I want these years to mean something, to help someone else."

She feels her mood darkening. What if it's all been for naught? Then she sees her drum.

"Look!" Janet says, pointing. "I got my drum out! The other night, my neighbors Gloria and Rosemary were here, and we played piano and sang. Johnny brought me asparagus. I love asparagus, even though I can't eat it. Since Steve, Steph, and Reid won't eat it, I gave it to the vegetarians next door. Gloria stopped by earlier today and brought these yellow irises. She tiptoed in while I was sleeping and laid them at my feet. I didn't think they were real.

"All these things help bring me out. And I love when you visit. Makes me laugh and calms me down."

"I am so glad. We do have fun, don't we?"

Next week, Janet will go for eyelid surgery to try to keep her lower lashes from rubbing her eye. Recently, she saw her "mouth man" who fitted her for teeth.

"Here," she says, "I'll show them to you. Steve says they look fine, and he never lies, but I think they look phony. The teeth aren't even in alignment and my mouth looks all crooked." She grimaces. "Yeah ...I don't know where I'll wear them. I can't talk any better, can't eat with them, and can't close my lips over them. And they are really hard to get in."

Janet pulls the prosthesis out of its pink box. Four small teeth, pearly and perfect, attached to a thin oblong plate—the device slender to better slide into her ravaged mouth.

Looking in the bathroom mirror, forcing her lips to part as much as they can, she shoves and twists the prosthesis, but can't get it in. "Ugh," she whispers. "What's the use."

She lets out a disgusted sigh and returns, holding them partially in her mouth. "See," she says, "they're just not right." She puts them back into their box and flops onto the couch, weariness melting her body into the upholstery.

"I don't like this," she says, pointing to her face. "But I am used to it now."

64

The News

Dotty

JUNE 2008

Steve calls me the evening after Janet's outpatient eyelid surgery. He tells me the surgeons have found tumors throughout the right side of her face.

Oh, Janet.

This is it.

The news you knew would arrive someday. The news I kept telling myself I wouldn't have to hear.

How can it be summer when days feel so short?

65

Just Plain Wrong

Janet

JUNE 2008

"I'll send an email to everyone," Steve tells Janet as they lie in bed. Numbness consumes her. All she wants to do is sleep—all night, all day—to hide from this horror.

"How did they get it so wrong?" Janet asks again, a question they have gone over and over since they heard the news yesterday. The surgeons and radiologists had continually reassured Steve and Janet that her facial changes, pain, and itching were all due to her past radiation and scarring.

Steve's email updates family and friends:

> *To say that this news is devastating is an understatement. We're still trying to adjust to this latest cliff we've fallen off.*
>
> *How this progression was missed by the radiologists for the last two years is beyond me. Right now, we're in constant communication with a number of doctors trying to plan next steps, if any. We know*

that given the apparent size and location of the recurrent tumor and the radiation Jan's already had, our options are very limited.

And it also seems that the revolution I had planned for cancer treatment based on Jan's progress to which I'd devoted a couple of years' worth of spare time may have been just plain wrong.

I wish I could be optimistic. But after nineteen years and all the sacrifices Jan's made and the challenges and pain she's had to endure, I'm a bit short on optimism.

Over the next week or two, we're going to sift through the wreckage and see if there are any next moves to make. As we learn more, I'll let you all know.

For now, please keep Jan in your thoughts and prayers. She just mentioned to me how much she appreciates them.

Turning over to try to sleep, Janet feels Steve slip out of bed, hears him head out the door, down the hall. Another headache, she thinks. I wish I wasn't the reason for his pain.

But this time, it isn't a headache but overwhelming hopelessness that sends Steve to the family room. Not one to ever need much sleep, he uses nights like this one to reboot. To prepare for what comes next. To breathe. To pray that he will know what to do.

66

Sorting it Out

Dotty

JUNE 2008

The next day, I visit Janet. We need to be together as she sorts this news.

"We brought Reid and Steph together last night and told them everything. About the new diagnosis, where all the tumors are. That I have a month, maybe a year, but maybe only a month."

"I am holding out for the year," I say.

Janet calls two weeks later to cancel our visit. She has to go for an MRI to see if the cancer is behind her right eye and in her brain. She says she is sleeping about twenty hours a day. She'll call when she gets her spirits up.

Our time withers. Visits will get shorter now, perhaps farther apart. I breathe prayers for her. With a tinge of guilt, but out of necessity, I very deliberately fold my grief into a small bundle. Stuff it in my back pocket. To be able to function. For my family, for myself, for Janet.

After the MRI, Steve calls with an update.

"It's a bit of a train wreck here," he says. "We're trying to figure out what's next. Her eye doesn't move well, she's falling more, and she often struggles for words.

"Oncologists are always willing to try something; radiologists feel if they can't fix it, don't do it. If we can't find anything to improve her quality of life, and if she doesn't want any life-extending treatments, then enough is enough. There's nothing else to do. It's a tough pill to swallow for someone like me who has tried for the last nineteen years."

When Janet was first diagnosed, both she and Steve drew up wills, neither wanting heroic measures to keep them alive. They wished to be as comfortable as possible, but to be given no extreme therapeutics as death approached.

"I am trying to be philosophical. Up until the last couple of years, it has been manageable. Jan was a fully participatory mom—fishing, swimming— she's been a great mom and wife. I'm greedy. I want nineteen more years.

"I am a moral absolutist, and I absolutely don't like this."

67

Trying to Find What's Lost

Janet

August 2008

The phone rings and Janet answers.

"Hi, Janet! How're ya doin' today?"

"Hi, Dotty. Things here are lousy. I just threw up and can't find the phone. I wanted to call Steve, but my leg didn't work, and I can't find the phone."

"I'll be right there."

"No, you don't have to come over. I'm fine. You have things to do. I'll be fine."

"I'm coming over."

We visit for two hours.

The missing phone—the family room phone Janet prefers—is found downstairs. She rarely goes down there anymore.

Sitting in her usual spot on the couch, Janet directs the thin orange hose attached to her squirt bottle toward her mouth. The hose was added recently to try to protect her raw nose. She can't see or feel that part of her face, and the constant jabbing with the squirt bottle makes her nose and upper lip bleed.

Her silky flowered pajamas belie her mood.

"I'm so frightened now," she says, "and I can tell that Steve is too." She squirts a little more Boost. Wipes up the spills on her chin with a soft cloth.

"I feel like I'm going crazy," she says.

She can't remember Steve's phone number. A number she has called several times a day for years.

"Here, Dotty," Janet says, handing over the notebook where now she writes copious notes—not as a journal, but to keep track of the daily details her memory cannot. "Could you write down Steve's numbers? I think they're on a note on the refrigerator, but I couldn't find it." She watches as his cell and work numbers get added in large letters and numbers even she can see.

Janet considers an upcoming family reunion.

"I don't want to go," Janet says," but I wonder if it will be the last chance I have to see my family. Except for Lynn and Donna, of course—they come down a lot."

Alternatives are discussed. She could go up early and rest for a full day or two. Then the day of the reunion, family could visit her at Lynn's house.

"But I don't want to feel like an old woman in a wheelchair," Janet says. "I used to do it all: play volleyball, throw Frisbees, toss horseshoes, eat and drink and talk."

In the end, she does not go.

Surgery is no longer an option; the tumors are too advanced. She's trying a new experimental inhibitor called Sorafenib, which her oncologist says has a 50 percent chance of preventing her tumors' growth.

She has stopped taking the every-four-hours morphine which caused excessive exhaustion. Now she wears a patch with a pain reliever good for three days. Anything that makes life easier is a plus.

Janet checks her blood pressure every few minutes, wondering if her dizziness is caused by high or low blood pressure. Or dehydration. Or hunger. Or the drugs, the tumors, or a combination of them all.

"I don't want to live until Christmas," she says. "It's too hard. Steve's mother keeps saying, 'You'll live to see Stephanie get married.'" She shakes her head. "I don't think so."

I know so, she thinks. Living is just too damn hard.

68

J'Anne

Dotty

SEPTEMBER 2008

Steve calls. Janet's closest friend since grade school, J'Anne, is coming to visit from Australia, and he and Janet want me to meet her. I head over, surprised that Steve is home on a weekday.

"Jan's having a tough day," he explains when I arrive. "She woke up disoriented, couldn't walk or talk well. It scared Steph. She couldn't get her mom out of bed before leaving for classes, so she called me to come home in the middle of the day."

"Call me next time, Steve. I can be here in minutes."

Janet is brushing her teeth—she just finished a Boost—and Steve and I wait for her to return.

"It would be easier in some ways if she had Alzheimer's," he says, "if she didn't know what was going on. Each day she says she wakes up and things are a little worse. Like being on a roller coaster, up and down, but the slope is always down.

"The other day, one of my co-workers said he couldn't imagine what it was like. I told him, 'It's as if, twenty years ago, someone shot a gun at us. And the bullet has been approaching, in slow motion, ever since. It's almost here now, and we can't dodge it.'"

Janet comes out in a thick white robe. "You look like a polar bear," I say, hugging her bones under the softness. She has struggled to stay warm; it's raining out, a nor'easter coming through. Steve tucks a quilt around her legs, drapes a cloud-covered blue fleece blanket over her shoulders. He puts drops in her eye, a bandage with antibiotic over her nose sore, and finger-combs her hair.

Then she scoots off to do something. She doesn't say what. Steve is used to this. "Where're you going, Speedy?"

When Janet returns, she tells me her sister Lynn and a friend were here over the weekend. "We went over to Rosemary's for six hours!" she says, with a laugh. "I think that's why I'm so bad. I overdid it. It was too much."

J'Anne arrives an hour later with her eighty-six-year-old mother. Both have beautiful, dyed red hair. They present Janet with pink roses and she jumps up to get a vase. I shoo her back to the couch and arrange the bouquet. Steve settles her under the blankets.

Janet drinks water, then pear nectar from her squirt bottles.

"I have trouble with aspiration because my epiglottis doesn't work," she tells J'Anne. "So I will probably die from pneumonia. But I think that's better than dying from cancer."

"You always said you'd outrun cancer and die of something else," says Steve, laughing. "Is this what you're planning?"

Steph comes home to a reception of shouts and hugs. Music is J'Anne's life now and she plays on Janet's recorder, then searches the piano bench for some sheet music she sent last Christmas. I snuggle next to Janet and Steph and we listen as J'Anne plays the piano; Steve and J'Anne's mother catch up in the other room.

J'Anne and Janet reminisce about playing in the drum and fife band. "Janet was the best drummer in the Northeast," says J'Anne.

"People called us the twins, Jan and J'Anne," says Janet. "We used to walk arm-in-arm down the street together..."

"...for miles!" adds J'Anne.

"...doing the Wizard of Oz walk," continues Janet. "Right, left, right, left, cross-over, hop back, switch feet."

They jump up to demonstrate. J'Anne links her silky-bloused arm with Janet's fuzzy white one, and together they become two giggling girls again, skipping without a care in the world.

69

Beer

Janet

SEPTEMBER 2008

It's midmorning, and Janet scuttles into her bedroom, Woody close behind. From the bottom drawer of her bureau, she pulls out an amber glass bottle tucked under a pile of nightgowns and plops onto the bed, arranging the pillows to support her back. Wrapping her hand in the sheet to protect it from the corrugated edges, she twists off the metal top, pours the liquid into the plastic squirt bottle she's brought from the kitchen, then sets the IPA bottle with its green Ballantine label on her bedside table. The same kind dad used to drink, she thinks. She squirts one sip, two, three into her mouth, and feels her body grow warm as she savors its bitterness. Another sip and all the sharp edges of pain and fright seem smoother.

Like a river carving a canyon. Or the way the ocean tumbles stones and shells and glass, rounding them round, round, round. So pretty and round, ground down round. She keeps sipping, tumbling with sea glass in soft pastels of greens, blues, and opaque clears. I love sea glass, she thinks as her eyes close. I used to collect it. I wonder where it all went?

She opens her eyes and glances at the clock. Yeah, I have time to hide it all before anyone comes home. She squirts in another sip, sets the plastic bottle beside the glass one, curls into the pillows, and relaxes into sleep.

Talking About Death

Dotty

OCTOBER 2008

Lunchtime, but my mind is not on my sandwich. Death consumes my thoughts. I haven't gotten used to death yet, especially with friends my age. Memories of past losses engulf me.

We were fourteen when my twin sister Patty and I stood on the step looking in the front door we had entered often, though not as often as the back door. On that day, however, we didn't know how to cross the threshold. Since we were born, this home had been a place of safety, of storybooks and silly games, of sleepovers and family birthday parties.

Now our Grammy lay in a hospital bed in the living room, and we couldn't move our feet. Our Grammy, who would stop all her chores—her cooking or canning or gardening—to read us Kimmy Kangaroo, the story we'd choose because it was the longest one in the book and gave us more time to sit on the couch with her between us, her softness cushioning any blow. But now she was mad.

"Go away, then," she said to us with a wave of her arm. Mom, standing by the side of her mother's bed, cajoled us to come see her, but we simply could not. A strange new anxiety rooted me. From the doorway, I waved, and said, "Goodbye." Grammy died the next day.

That moment still haunts me. Why didn't I go in? Perhaps love was the reason. Fear of losing her kept me away.

Grammy died of cancer, as Grandpa would four years later, alone in his living room—though Mom visited every day and he had round-the-clock care. When Patty and I were forty, Dad died of aplastic anemia, screaming in pain, Mom at his side in the ER cubicle. I was not there with any of them. My continual prayer is to be with Mom, holding her hand when she dies.

In my early thirties, my fear of death changed. It took a dying elderly friend and a toddler to show me its beauty and natural presence in our lives.

Seven years before Dad died, I was pregnant and Ruth had just turned two. Jonathan and I learned that a beloved family friend, Helen Norwood, our closest neighbor in New Hampshire, was dying. We hopped on a plane.

Helen lay under wool blankets in her living room, her cheeks gaunt, but her eyes bright and clear. Surrounded by partially finished Pebble People, her bird and animal creations, she recounted her delight in traveling the world and in combing the beaches from New England to Nova Scotia, and at her winter home in Florida to collect the perfect stones for each sculpture: turtles, cats, penguins, dolphins. For our wedding, she made Jonathan and me a large exquisite one-of-a-kind owl, then a tiny one for our first anniversary.

Now as we spoke, Helen pointed to one of her more basic but most treasured works of art: a stone crèche, complete with manger, kings, shepherds, and sheep, and a tiny shell Jesus on a cupped stone bed watched over by the simple curves of Mary and Joseph. "I want Ruth to have it now," she said. Helen had loved Ruth since her birth, and they had bonded the previous summer playing with craft supplies.

In her final days, Helen experienced a new kind of travel: leaving her body, then returning. Her eyes glimmered as she spoke of the beauty she had seen and her excitement at this new adventure.

Our little Ruth understood. When we told her Helen was in heaven, our little girl drew her a picture, then took it outside to hold up in the air. "Mrs. Norwood," Ruth said. "She's a diamond in the sky."

Today, Janet and I explore this new territory.

Janet snuggles into the fuzziness of her robe and blanket as I read "Entering Death," a poem by John O'Donohue, hoping his consoling words and blessings will bring her comfort. I continue in *Anam Cara,* reading passages on fear, which consumes so much of her thought now.

"This gives me a lot to think about," she rasps. "I want to not be so afraid, but don't know how."

Can O'Donohue's Celtic wisdom and gentle counsel hold any meaning for Janet? Or anything I say?

I turn the conversation to relinquishing control.

With the last dregs of Janet's energy dwindling, her sight minimal, and her long fight against cancer ending, she's lost all control of her body. She takes charge where she can, directing her family to vacuum here, clean up there, rearrange, fix, help.

Her hunger for order resonates with me. On my worst days, the house needs to be clean. I pick up piles, sweep the floor, pay bills. Everything must be organized before I can rest.

This perspective is hard for her constantly badgered family to maintain. Everyone is grieving, but frustration sets in as her demands increase.

"Maybe, Janet, this is time to simply love," I suggest. "You don't have to worry about the day-to-day details anymore. You can spend your energy on simply being with your family.

She nods. "I'll try," she says.

How hard it must be to simply do anything.

"I do feel like Steve and I are getting closer," she says.

I admire how in love they've remained despite all these years of illness. "Poe's poem, 'Annabelle Lee,' reminds me of you two," I say, and recite...

> But our love it was stronger by far
>   than the love
> Of those who were older than we—
> Of many far wiser than we—
> And neither the angels in heaven above,
> Nor the demons down under the sea,
> Can ever dissever my soul from the soul
> Of the beautiful Annabel Lee...

Janet nods, linking her husband with the grieving poet. "Steve always knows how to fix things, but he told me the other day, 'I don't like to leave anything undone. So I can't believe I have run out of options for the one person that means the most to me.'"

A Fight

Janet

NOVEMBER 2008

Janet calls Lynn.

"I have to tell you what's going on around here," Janet says. "Last night, Steve and I had a fight.

"'Why do you keep calling me names?' I asked him when he came in to go to bed.

"'What are you talking about?' he said as if he didn't know.

"'Before, when you were in the kitchen, you said I'm an ogre and unreasonable.'

"'Jan, I never said that.'

"Lynn, I am sure to God he said it several times. He got very angry—you know how he gets—that temper showing again.

"'I'm getting out of here,' he said. 'You call me a liar, accuse me of saying I called you an ogre. You're out of it! You're nuts!' Then he stormed out the bedroom door and shut it...hard. He went right downstairs all night. I guess to go on the computer or watch TV. He also said how dare I call him a liar, and this after he calls me worse names all the time.

"Lynn, what I'm telling you are not lies. These are just the facts that I am trying to clear up and figure out."

72

Allegations

Janet

November 2008

"Don't touch me! Stop it! Steve, you're hurting me!"

"Jan, calm down, what are you talking about?"

"Stop hitting me! Help! Somebody!"

"Jan, it's one a.m., you'll wake Steph. What is the matter with you?"

Janet flings herself out of bed and tears down the hall to the living room. Steve follows. Janet lurches for the phone, but Steve gets there first.

"Give me that phone, Steve. I'm calling the police."

For two hours, Janet rages at Steve. Whenever he comes near her, she pummels him with her fists. Her fury is boundless.

"I know you've been sleeping around. My god, Steve! You've been sleeping with Steph!"

"Jan, you're crazy! I absolutely have not."

"Don't lie to me."

"Jan, just let me hold you. Here, sit on the couch with me."

"Oh no. I'm not coming near you," Janet hisses, huddling on the floor. Woody curls next to her.

"Let me get you a blanket. You must be cold."

"Get away from me. Just get away. Call Lynn, call Donna. I am leaving. I am going to Rosemary's. I will not stay in this house."

"It's the middle of the night, Jan. They're all sleeping. You can call them in the morning."

"Just stay away, Steve. I don't trust you. I can't believe I ever trusted you. Look at these bruises. You don't hit people you love. Our marriage is a fraud. I don't believe you ever really loved me."

Finally, her energy sags. She drags herself to the couch and dozes lightly but keeps an eye on Steve, who sits at the far end of the other couch.

As dawn breaks, she dresses in jeans and a T-shirt, tosses other clothes and toiletries in a bag, and heads for the door to walk over to Rosemary's.

"I am not going to live in a house where I am physically abused. If you try to come and get me, I will call the police."

Palpable Sadness

Dotty

NOVEMBER 2008

Bright rays sharpen Janet's edges as she paces Rosemary's sunroom floor. Lynn and Donna sit together on a couch against the far wall, shoulders touching in a united front. I try to imagine the phone call they received from Janet yesterday, their drive down.

"He threw me on the bed three times," Janet rants. "He punched me in the crotch. What husband does that? Look at these bruises."

She strides toward me, lifts her shirt, pulls down the waistband of her jeans. I see no bruises.

"He lies, tells the kids I hate them, says I insult them. He tells me I am insane. He yelled at me, saying I try to make him suffer like me."

She sits, tired from her rage. "But it's my fault. I praised him too much, praised him all the time for the help with doctors and for loving me. But look where it has led. He said if I call the abuse hotline I will end up in an insane asylum." She storms into the next room.

"Three times he punched me," she calls, "threw me down. Look at these bruises. I am never going back there."

I listen. Do not judge. I can't. I was not there. Steve called earlier and told me what had happened, that Janet had accused him of hurting her, that she was at Rosemary's. So here I am. To be with her. To listen as she sits, jumps up, paces, sits, paces.

Stephanie spends the next two nights at our house.

Two days later, Steve calls. His voice weary.

"I found out why the doxycycline hasn't been able to control the tumors," he says. "Jan's been drinking alcohol. She didn't tell me. What does alcohol do to this antibiotic? Makes it not work."

Janet knew. She had been told over and over by her doctors and by Steve that she could not drink any form of alcohol.

"I had some suspicions based on her mood changes, but couldn't prove it. I started searching while she was at Rosemary's."

Steve and Reid found and removed alcohol from all over the house. They filled two car trunks.

"We found beer hidden in socks in her drawer," Steve says. "Bottles throughout closets, tucked behind pots and pans. I went down in the basement where we have a pantry full of food—Reid's friends call it the Zombie Apocalypse Pantry; we buy in bulk when there's a sale—and I noticed the one-gallon bottles of Wesson cooking oil. Yellow, yellow, clear, clear, clear. Took the tops off. Alcohol.

"The psychologist who is working with Jan says it is very common for people who are desperate and depressed to escape by using alcohol.

"I didn't know until it was too late."

Three days later, Janet and Steve stand in their front yard, arms entwined behind each other's back. I hesitate, unsure what to say.

"Everything is okay now," Steve says, but my eyes are on Janet. She nods.

"It's okay," she says. "I'm coming back home."

I hug them both. What else can I do?

74

Seekers of Intangibles

Dotty

NOVEMBER 2008

What do I do with the sadness of others? With my own sadness?

I contemplate all that grieves me.

My friend Elaine has breast cancer. She is undergoing chemo and was on my mind last month as a rocking whale-watching boat off Monterey, California flipped my stomach into rare seasickness. Though the whales and birds buoyed me, my main focus was getting to solid unmoving ground. Elaine did not have that choice; her nausea would not subside even when she curled on her office floor. Hers lasted and lasted.

The day before Thanksgiving, up in our family house in North Wolfeboro, New Hampshire, Jonathan's defibrillator went off. His mother was there. I was running errands. He had been making chocolate candies—his dad's famous booze balls—

and sat down for some tea. The next thing he knew he was on his back. His first thought: Huh, my defibrillator must have gone off. His second thought: Wow. I didn't feel a thing. Then, the terror. Why did it go off? Will it go off again?

He spent four days in the local New Hampshire hospital's ICU, missing the family dinner. After his release, he was forbidden to drive until he saw his cardiologist in Maryland. So getting us back home was up to me. On Thanksgiving Saturday, I drove us three hours to Mom's in Massachusetts; on Sunday, drove us home to Annapolis in the pouring rain. A drive that normally takes eight hours took twelve.

Though we used to switch off about every three hours on long trips, in recent years, Jonathan has taken over the bulk of our long-distance driving. We have a ritual. He starts driving, and about twenty minutes into the trip, I say, "I can drive anytime." "Okay, good to know," he says, then drives for hours, only letting me take over briefly so he can nap. I haven't driven for hours at a stretch in over a decade.

This time, that option wasn't possible, and there was no time for exhaustion or sadness or fear. Not yet. I was in crisis mode; this job was mine alone. Though Jonathan felt fine, the same thought lingered inside both of us: Why did his heart stop again? Later, doctors would weigh in with their hypotheses. But on this drive, I silently offered my prayer of thanks to his defibrillator, My Little Friend.

In the sixth hour of the drive, and nowhere near home, I told Jonathan, "I have immense internal fortitude," a phrase repeating like a mantra in my head as the relentless downpour made the highway and clog of traffic hard to see. Sometimes another mantra showed up—I have dogged determination— my go-to whenever one foot must be put in front of the other, even when everything inside me is gone. In emergencies, calm takes over; my anxiety is put off until later. Whatever needs to be done, I do; whatever decisions must be made, I make.

My mettle faltered only once on that twelve-hour drive—with a thirty-second pity party in a rest stop bathroom stall on the New Jersey Turnpike. A hard, "poor-me" silent cry. Then I was good to go.

This same stoicism works with sadness. Though occasionally okay for the ill person to see my sorrow, I don't want to call attention to it. No one should be comforting me when they are the ones who are hurting. "You can cry to me," I tell them, "I'm here to listen." No spouting of platitudes; no advice given unless asked, and even then, with caution. I cannot fix their illness, but I can walk with them through it.

Alone, I cry out my sadness for them, then tuck it away to better support them and myself.

I'm not good at accessing my own personal sadness; too practiced at sequestering it away. I hide from it with a positive outlook, couched hopefully in reality and not in the clouds. But there is value in diving into my well of despair. Not to bathe or wallow in, but to access it. By acknowledging my own sorrows, I can better understand the deep well of another person's sadness, better understand their grief, whether they've lost a loved one or their own cherished selves.

Because Janet and I deal with our own limitations, our empathy for each other carries a greater depth of understanding. We both wish our lives hadn't taken a dive—hers exponentially more devastating than mine—and landed us underwater, but because of our journeys with illness, we see others who struggle with different eyes.

Janet and I don't talk much about our determination, our internal fortitude. We don't have to. It's evident in the way we live our lives. I think that's what's made it easy to be with her, to stick by her even as cancer invades her brain.

Some people drain my energy; others bolster it. Janet has been somewhere in between. She offers not just her own brand of toughness but also a place of peace, where she understands me and I understand her. We don't have to dwell on it; in each other's presence, we feel nurtured. Though the cancer is altering her sense of peace, which has begun adding tension to our meetings, our visits continue.

Why keep showing up? What do I get from Janet? Unconditional friendship. She has helped me to transition into life with chronic illness. Janet always welcomes me into her home as I am on that day. She lets me feel crummy and tired or giddy and fine. Her Catholic soul and my Quaker soul have found common ground in kindness and love—of each other, of friends and family, of nature. The woods and the water feed us, the birds lighten our spirits. Our chats feel deeper than the mere trading of stories. We bare ourselves to each other. Admit foibles. Lay open fears. Talk of death.

We both, like many, are seekers of intangibles. On the water, we look for solace, joy, freedom, beauty. On hiking treks, I seek the deep silence only the mountains hold. Over and over, Janet has reached for hope and relied on faith.

But she and we all have very tangible bodies. Ones with their own agendas. Our bodies don't listen to our lofty dreams, don't care about the grace that feeds us or the children we seek to nurture. We must find our way in spite of them.

Janet's courage has been tested and found true, and I, simply by being with her, have been lifted. Our meetings have helped to alleviate our sadness by offering compassion and hefty doses of humor. She's never pulled the "poor-me" card around me, though I know she feels it. All who deal with illness must pull that card sometimes—even if it's silently in a public bathroom stall. It is how we survive.

75

Jekyll

Dotty

JANUARY 2009

Low winter sun lays a wide trace of shadows across Janet's front lawn, their chill crawling under my sweatshirt. Indoors, the shadows linger.

Janet has shrunk below eighty pounds, her body truly skeletal. The cold lives inside her bones. She piles on three blankets as she nestles into the couch. A bandaid covers her eroding nose.

Today Janet can whisper; yesterday she had no voice at all.

"It scares me," she says, pointing to her throat. She suspects cancer skulks there as well. Each loss is visceral, another insult. Every night, Steve patches her ulcerated eye with plastic wrap, then pulls down a fleece band to hold the patch in place. Underneath, ointment bathes her eye, keeping it moist. Her eyelid no longer closes when she sleeps.

I squeeze a small line of gel across her eye in a ritual we repeat every visit.

Then Janet wrestles out of her blanket and jumps up, her quick change of mood amusing me.

"I have something to show you," she calls as she darts down the hall. She knows every corner and shadow in this house and moves easily, unhindered by her limited vision.

"Look what I got," she says, grinning as she comes back from her bedroom. She holds out a new pair of pale yellow Mary Jane Crocs. "Very stylish," I tell her as she slips them on over her bulky green socks.

Woody lounges at our feet, where we pat him for long minutes, his long dark coat silky soft, but I can feel the lumps. Soon, he'll have his own surgery to remove lipomas—fatty, non-cancerous growths on his back and ribs that have become painful when he lies down. Even her dog cannot escape the vagaries of health.

Zippy eases the afternoon along, and I tell Janet about writing the author, Haven Kimmel, to let her know how much we were enjoying her book.

"You also should have sent her a picture of me," Janet whispers, "so that she would understand. But I don't know. Maybe not.

"I had an out-of-town friend drop by soon after my eye was removed. When she got ready to leave, she asked to take a picture of me. I told her I really didn't want my picture taken, but she insisted and took it anyway. I cried for a long time after she left."

There are no photos of Janet and me.

After our dose of *Zippy*, after we share our see-you-again-soon hugs at the door, I drive home, thinking about my friend. Two thoughts dominate her mind right now, beyond her worries for her children. She wants others to know her story so that maybe Steve's research and her path through cancer might help others who face this disease. She also fears being forgotten; she is saddened to think she has lived through all this, only to vanish, her story unknown.

No one can fully understand the enormity of what those with cancer face each day, what Janet has faced for the last twenty years. Even her family, there daily, cannot know all she is feeling. Each person is alone in their illness, she more trapped than most.

I can walk into the world, as can others with hidden illnesses, and pretend to be fine. But Janet is trapped behind her face, which she feels has become grotesque. Her exuberant pre-cancer spirit was quashed bit by bit as surgeries contorted her appearance, and she hid more often from staring eyes. Only the few people she trusts—her family, some of her neighbors, a few friends—still get to see her delight, her sense of play and fun, and feel her love.

76

Hyde

Dotty

"Aaarr," Janet growls in her husky rasp a week later, trying to tell me something but frustrated again as words hide in the recesses of her tumor-invaded brain. The cruel complexity of cancer's rampant takeover of the mind, however, goes beyond capturing words. It distorts personality. Janet fights hard to be herself, but at times the beast emerges, and she hurls a stream of invective no child, or husband, or sister should have to hear. They know it's the cancer talking, but it speaks with her voice. The knife-edged vitriol cuts deep; a fiendish twist amidst so much love.

Today, I meet the not-Janet. We lounge on our couches while I read to her. Suddenly, she jumps up.

"I've got to get something," she says and scurries to her bedroom.

After waiting five minutes, I go in to see if she wants any help.

"Get out of here," she hisses. "What are you doing in here? Get out!"

I hurry down the hall, holding back tears, having

glimpsed what her family lives with every day and every night.

Janet returns, bustles about in the kitchen, opening drawer after drawer.

"I have got to find glasses that work," Janet says. "I can't stand not being able to find ones that work. I think Steve hides them. He probably does it on purpose."

Janet keeps searching—for her squirt bottles, her medication. Finally, she sits down and grabs her notebook, pushes it into my lap.

"Look at all the mean things my family says to me," she says. "I write them down, so I won't forget. They call me horrible names, make fun of me behind my back. They think I can't hear them, but I can."

I listen, look at the notebook. Nod.

"Look," she says, handing me a different scrap of paper with scrawled writing. "I rewrote my will. I want the doctors to do whatever it takes. I don't want to die. I am afraid to die. I told Steve, and he said okay. He watched me sign it."

I listen, look at the paper. Nod.

Finally, she settles into her blankets on the couch. I finish the *Zippy* chapter. Tranquility, for a few moments, returns.

Later, at the door, we hug as always. "See you next week," we say.

In the car, I sit for a few minutes, breathing away the tension that pervades her house now. Recently, I have found it both hard to leave and hard to stay.

77

Not a Person

Janet

FEBRUARY 2009

Fresh from lipoma surgery, Woody limps inside and flumps onto the family room rug. Bandages cover his back and his front paw.

"Oh Woody," Janet says, kneeling on the floor beside him, patting his head. "I missed you so much. I am so glad you're okay."

Then Janet settles onto the couch. Steve pours liquid food and medicines into the feeding tube she abhors.

"I'm not a person anymore," she says to Steve. "All this stuff hanging out of me."

After he finishes and goes to the kitchen to clean up, Janet calls to him. "Are you sure that's enough food? I don't feel full."

Steve knows he can't overfeed her. The doctors have told him if he gives her too much, she will bloat and get infections in her stomach.

"Steve? Steve! Are you trying to starve me?"

She weighs seventy-two pounds.

78

You

Dotty

FEBRUARY 2009

After visiting Janet, I take refuge on the beach.

The water's blue-green against the pale brown sand and the stillness of the late afternoon make it feel like being inside a photograph. The perfect calm of the water draws me to the horizon where gray-blue meets misty white, where two container ships sit like cardboard cutouts plunked there by a child.

The tundra swans are not here today and I miss their trilling, their congenial humming, their brazen hooting. I came seeking their clamor, hoping they would connect me to this world, to make the unreal more real.

Today I finally ventured inside myself to a place I have been hiding.

My dearest Janet, I say silently to myself and to her, I know you are dying.

You have survived so long I somehow fooled myself into believing I wouldn't have to say goodbye.

But today, you have begun to leave. You are still feisty in your scarecrow bones, but I could see the pain feasting on your body. You didn't laugh when I read *Zippy*.

I have never, in all our visits, burst into tears as I walked out the door.

Today, I did.

After I finished *Zippy*—almost—two more pages, and promised to get Kimmel's next book; after you looked for your morphine and couldn't find it; after your hospice nurse arrived; after Steve began getting you comfortable again on the couch (you had jumped up to turn on the light for the nurse—the sliding door curtains closed because Woody kept barking, sent to the porch after throwing up all over the rug); after I hugged you, then hugged you again and promised to be back next week; after you said (in your croaky whispery voice that has become almost impossible to understand, but I heard this) "I love you," and I said, "I love you;" after I gathered up my coat and purse and book and Steve caught my eye and mouthed "Thank you," and I knew he meant it, I pulled on my boots, opened the door, and broke into a sob.

I stopped at the library to get out Kimmel's next book about her mother, ironically titled, *She Got Up Off the Couch*. Got it a week early to be sure we had it. Wondering not whether we will have enough time to finish the book (we won't), but whether I will need to renew it, twice; whether we will still be meeting—me reading, you curled on the couch listening—in April.

And so I have come to the beach to look for the tundra swans from Alaska. But all that float by are the mute swans, their silence keeping me inside the photograph where I try to believe in beauty again. The sun dips behind the clouds and the blue-green water turns gray. The wind blows cold, kicking up chop.

No gulls call from the pilings; no ducks fly overhead. Feeling as empty as the skies, I drift back to my car.

The Shocker

Janet

FEBRUARY 2009

Tucked back in her bedroom, Janet grins at Donna and vigorously rubs her pink fleece blanket between her hands. When Lynn peeks in to see if Janet is asleep, Janet touches the blanket to Lynn's arm. Sparks crackle.

"Ah!" Lynn cries. "You're shocking me! Donna, make her stop!"

Janet and Donna giggle like they did so long ago.

"Go get your husband," Lynn suggests.

Janet walks down the hall, her body as wispy as her hair, but her eye glints as her hands move briskly inside the blanket. Steve sprawls on the couch, watching a game.

"Here comes the Shocker," says Donna.

Donna holds Janet steady as she leans toward Steve and rubs his head with the blanket.

"Hey, I got a head scratch out of it," he says. But he doesn't laugh. He finds very little to laugh about these days.

Janet rubs his whole face, then leans down and kisses him. Then she turns toward Donna, and together they laugh when the charged fleece shocks them both. They embrace, Donna whispering, "I love you." With unintelligible words, but complete clarity, Janet responds in kind.

80

On This Snowy Day With You, Dear Janet

Dotty

MARCH 2009

I visit you in the hospital. Double pneumonia and an E. coli infection. Your whisper is barely decipherable now.

"One thing after another," you croak.

"Janet, I think your body is trying to tell you something," I say.

You nod, then write me messages.

Steve says I'll go home soon. Lynn says I need to go to hospice.

Rubbing your leg, I tell you we don't need to talk.

I am just glad that on this snowy day, we are both here.

1

Last Days

Janet

MARCH 2009

Pale beech leaves tremble in the breeze, a fragile shimmery rustling. They have held on all winter, but now they begin to fall.

The Stella Maris hospice house evaluator, a burly ex-D.C. policeman, visits Janet and Steve at home on the day she is released from the hospital.

"Listen, I know I can do better," Steve tells him. "I just have to figure out some things so I can work more from home during the day. I can do this."

Patting Steve's shoulder with his large but gentle hand, the evaluator says, "Son, you don't understand. You are so far over your head you can't see it. The time has long since passed for you to do this.

"Look, it's called respite. You need to let us take Janet up to the hospice house, so you and your family can get a break. This is hard for everyone, including Janet. I do this for a living. I know. You are way over your head here, Steve. Let's just give everyone a break."

Traces of snow still cover the lawn as Janet walks unaided down the driveway to the waiting transport ambulance. Spruce as always in jeans and flowery shirt, she defies the cold, her black coat flying, open to the wind. A mourning dove tries to set a desolate mood, but Janet will have none of that. She climbs in and sits on the stretcher, sneakers—the shoes Steve couldn't tie because her feet are too swollen—pointed up. Janet doesn't say goodbye to anyone. She doesn't speak at all.

They're just trying to get rid of me, she thinks. Sending me to an institution. They think I'm crazy.

Lynn, unable to bear her sister being alone, follows her to the Stella Maris hospice house. Steve, heeding the evaluator's advice, stays home.

Lynn and Janet wander the halls, rest. One night, Lynn turns on a video camera. "Let's send a message to Donna," she suggests.

Ha! Janet thinks. I know what to do.

She powers every ounce of herself to the surface, and for a few moments, the true Janet reigns. The one who swam and played and fished with Steph and Reid throughout their childhood; the one who made up silly songs about her family at Christmas; the one who loved to throttle the *Janet P* into top gear and fly across the Chesapeake Bay; the one who just last summer put aside her inhibitions and health concerns and sat with Steve on a grassy hillside at Annapolis's Quiet Waters Park, rocking out with her favorite bluesmen, Baltimore's own Kelly Bell Band.

Decked out in her red robe, arms akimbo, Janet grins, then flaps her elbows, hops, turns, bends, and wiggles her butt in a Chicken Dance.

"Hi, Donna," she croaks, a light of laughter shining around her. She crosses her arms over her chest, then points toward the camera. Toward Donna. And mouths the words she wants Donna to hear. "I love you."

Four days later, the doctors feel she is stable enough to go home.

Donna comes down to celebrate her return from the hospital and hospice. But nothing is easy. Janet does not feel like celebrating. Time is short.

At 11:30 one night, Steve irons his shirts, enough for the next two weeks. At midnight, he washes dishes and wipes down the kitchen counters. Janet shuffles back and forth behind him, stabbing at a note she's just written.

"It's time for freakin' bed," he says, exasperated. "I've already done two loads of laundry."

But Janet knows there is still another load in the basement. She paces, spouts incoherently, scrawls frantically on her pad of paper.

The Stella Maris evaluator returns the next afternoon to determine she needs to return to the hospice house. When he leaves, Janet is frantic. She stomps around the living room, then flies into the bathroom. "Trying to kill me!" she bellows. She flings up the window and before Lynn and Steve can arrive, hoists one leg over the window ledge, straddles the sill, her foot dangling two stories up, and begins shouldering her way outside, away from her tormentors.

Lynn bear-hugs her under the arms and hauls her back in as Janet flails and growls.

"Janet, jeez, c'mon! No one is trying to kill you!" Lynn tries to hug her once she is safe in the bathroom, but Janet pulls away, sneering. With a deep, ragged breath, she pulls back her right arm, then powers her fist forward, a knuckle-on-bone punch straight into Lynn's head.

Later, Janet stops pacing to gaze out into the darkness obscuring the backyard and marsh. Momentarily lucid, she turns to Lynn. "I am going to die soon."

The next morning the transport ambulance arrives. Raving and incoherent, Janet spouts disjointed tirades, ferociously swats the attendants as they wrestle her onto the gurney. Working efficiently, they strap her down. Steve comes over to stand by her before they load her into the ambulance. She glares up at him. "Look what you've done to me. I can't believe you are doing this to me," she says. Her longest articulate sentences in weeks. The last words Steve will hear.

82

Farewell to You, Dear Janet

Dotty

MARCH 2009

A family trip to New Mexico has kept me apart from Janet. Back home, I wake this morning to my heart pounding, preparing for the inevitable. Then, the call from Lynn I have been dreading yet worried I'd miss. My stomach drops, but in the background, Lynn says, "I'll be right there, Janet." Whew... there's time. Lynn says the nurse told her it will be in the next few hours. "I'm leaving now," I say. "I'll be there in one."

Through much of the long drive around the Beltway to the north of Baltimore, I hold Janet present, speaking to her perhaps for the last time. Tears stream, but my voice does not falter.

It's okay to leave, Janet. You have fought this for so long, now it is okay to start your next journey. No more pain, no more suffering. Just peace. You can be yourself again. Leave the husk of your body behind. God called for you twenty years ago, and you said no. Now it's okay to say yes. Go to your mother and father. You have seen your children into college. You have been a good mom, a good wife, a good friend. We will be fine. You have my blessing, Janet, and my love. It's okay. It's okay. I am on my way. I will be there soon.

Through the last half hour of Beltway traffic, I silently pray my way to you.

The Stella Maris driveway seems endless. At last, I bolt out of the car, running with just enough awareness to hear a fish crow squawk. Down the long corridor to the elevator I hurry, enduring the ride to the fourth floor, to your room.

But you are gone, Lynn tells me. I am half an hour too late.

Your hands in mine are still warm, dear Janet. Black rosary beads entwine your fingers; two small scapulars lay tucked in your palm. I weep onto your fingers, kissing them, hoping you heard my voice, my words, my blessing.

The end was peaceful. Both your sisters were with you, Lynn, Donna and her husband Bob, your neighbor Rosemary. You knew I was on my way to see you, Lynn tells me. You were resting, sleeping, when Donna realized that you were no longer breathing. The angels took you in peace: a benevolent final gift.

Yesterday afternoon, after your rage and mania calmed, your family was here. Steve, Reid, and Steph had time to say goodbye to you.

This morning, Steve is too late. "I knew she'd do it when I wasn't here," he says.

Ah, death. The storybook endings are for storybooks.

We leave him with you. He sits by your head, smoothing back wisps of hair and caressing your ear, so lonely on the left side of your face. He must go to the funeral home but doesn't want to leave. I know the feeling. Sitting with your body keeps you here. When we leave, you'll be gone.

Then I have time alone with you, to hold your hand and kiss your forehead, now going cool, but still so soft.

I hope you heard me, Janet, I whisper. *I'm so sorry to have missed you.*

I've been praying for you. A week ago, at an old church you would have loved, Santuario de Chimayo, near Santa Fe, built in 1816, I placed a stone for you on a cross in the garden where people ask for miracles. I prayed, knowing you only needed one more miracle... to let go.

Your hands are so pale and delicate, your nails just hinting at the blue of forget-me-nots.

I promise I will not forget you. I will not let you be forgotten.

Peacefulness surrounds you. Free, finally released. How joyful that freedom must feel.

I cry for myself, for my loneliness; I cry for you, for how grueling your life had to be.

It's hard to leave, but it's time.

Not wanting you to be alone, and not wanting to be here when the funeral home people arrive, I am grateful when Lynn and Donna return. Walking on shaky legs out the long corridor, I acknowledge no one. But I hear one woman telling another she worries the Brussels sprouts in her refrigerator will not be okay while she is away.

I burst into the sun, and again the fish crow squawks. In the warm car, I shiver in my sweaty clothes. Call Jonathan and cry. On the drive home, high clouds move in and veil the sun, tempering the day. I make one stop, at the library, to return Kimmel's book about her mother, and realize I was right.

We didn't have enough time.

epilogue

Rhythms

Dotty

MARCH 2009

I rise early to walk through wonderland. Fluffs of snow sit like two-inch hats on each sweetgum ball. Every branch, every holly leaf, every tissue paper-thin leftover beech leaf is festooned. In the field, a beacon of sun slices through the clouds and illuminates a copse of trees, the wet bark and shimmering snow vibrant against the dark blue sky.

A black vulture flies over, the outer third of its wings white as though they've been dipped in snow paint. A hundred robins jump and flutter in a sun-melted spot, tossing damp leaf litter for worm prizes.

I take so many photos. If only that act alone could make it stay.

By noon, wonderland is gone.

With the coming of spring, I long for the wood thrush's haunting woodland melody. Using its two syrinxes simultaneously, the wood thrush can sing two different songs at the same time, his elaborate ethereal sound ringing through the trees.

In her last months, as cancer invaded her brain, the fear of dying accompanied by paranoia and delusion changed not only how Janet acted but also how she approached the end. She sang two songs. "I want to live!" she cried, scrawling a new will asking doctors to use extreme measures to keep her alive. And yet she drank, knowing the alcohol would prevent the doxycycline from working and allow the tumors to grow, knowing any liquid she drank would get into her lungs and could cause pneumonia. Trying to soothe pain and discomfort is primal; in desperate times, rational thinking and best-laid plans go to hell.

Hindsight can find us questioning our motives, our judgment, and our actions. Multiple cancer treatment options make every decision loom in complexity. Few choices are simple. So many factors to weigh: longevity, side effects, quality of life.

Years from now, will Steve question whether every step chosen in his pursuit was the best course. Probably. Did Janet wish she had decided against some of the treatments and surgeries? Chosen a different path? Sometimes. Hindsight allows us to evaluate whether the best decisions were made but cannot change their course. At each juncture, Steve and Janet found the most viable options, evaluated them, and made the best decisions they could for her welfare and the family's. It's all any of us can do.

Later in the week, the Bay calls me to go paddling. My kayak slices through water dented like hammered silver by faint gusts of breeze. The Bay is mine; no other boaters in sight. Bufflehead males puff and swagger for disinterested females. Horned grebes swim in packs of twos and threes. Wave after wave of Canada geese fill the air with their clamorous honking, heading north in multiple Vs. The tundra swans gather close to puff, preen, and hoot as they prepare for their journey. I rejoice today in their singing for soon these waterfowl will move on, a steady vacating of winter sojourners. Now the first osprey has returned, the first tree swallow.

With each season, I say goodbye. With each season, I greet returners. I need these birds. Their rhythms, their predictable patterns. They, like nothing else, help ease my sorrow.

My visits with Janet fill my heart. Connecting with Janet, talking about fear, frustration, longing, death, allowed me to see not just her vulnerability but also my own. Not just her strength, but mine. I never once doubted her strength. Despite her family nicknames of Puny Head and China Doll, she was a force to be reckoned with.

She never backed down from what she felt was the right direction to travel. As a child, she forged her own path, drumming rather than playing the fife, and finding ways to calm her rebellious siblings when

Donna used her stout body to block Lynn's *Howdy Doody* show. In a famous family quote, her resolve is clear: "You cannot ride my bicycle. Even if I say you can, you can't." When cancer thought it could beat her, she took it on.

She taught me being tough didn't mean you couldn't be soft; being open to vulnerabilities didn't make you a weakling.

John O'Donohue's words in *Anam Cara* resonate: "To be wholesome, we must remain truthful to our vulnerable complexities." For most of my life, it was unimaginable that I would be brave enough to allow myself to be vulnerable. But by delving for my truth—a continual journey—I am available on a deeper, more empathic level for others.

My time with Janet gave me a safe place to do what had eluded me: to feel worthy again. We nourished each other and found within our visits a place to be our best selves. The opportunity to share our honest and open hearts made each of us more whole.

Now I paddle the ripples, a sun orb glowing beside me, my companion on the chilly greenish gray water. On shore, a fish crow flies onto a treetop branch and utters its sore-throat sound, *uh-uhn, uh-uhn.*

Fish crows connect me to Janet. We listened to them on our kayak adventures, and they were there when she died, calling as I entered and left the hospice house. Several years from now, after many edits of this book, I will find inspiration for a better approach and begin writing this current version.

Within minutes of sitting down at my desk, two fish crows will fly into my yard, perch on the fence outside my study, and call.

Neither Janet nor I realized the gifts she would bestow upon me when she asked me to write her story. She gave me the gift of her trust by allowing me to enter even more fully into her life. She gave me purpose: the opportunity to write and share her journey with others.

But then came the additional and unexpected gift. By writing her story, I also wrote mine, entering more completely into my new self.

Dip, pull, dip, pull. The rhythm of paddling takes me from bustle to stillness, to a place where my heart has a voice. With the natural world as solace, with birds as fuel, I move forward.

Acknowledgments

Writing a book is both singular and communal. I could not have done this alone. Each of these people added immeasurably to its creation.

In March 2008, I told Janet of a new memoir about a man's journey with cancer. Her response: "Would you write mine?"

Thus this book began. But, in actuality, it had started years before.

In 2003, when continuing to teach became impossible due to complications from MS, I floundered for months, wondering what to do. Kayaking led to writing on little scraps of paper, which led to a collection of early essays, which I (bravely!) took to the Ministry of Writing for Publication course taught by Tom Mullen at Pendle Hill, a Quaker retreat center in Wallingford, Pennsylvania.

Tom, former dean of Earlham School of Religion, professor, and much beloved Quaker author, became my first writing coach, showing me how humor, heart, and one's truth were the foundations for writing with purpose. His mentoring emboldened me to believe I could be a worthy writer, and I spent the next year developing a manuscript based on my kayaking forays on the Chesapeake Bay and into my world with multiple sclerosis.

Elizabeth Knight offered editorial advice and guidance on this fresh manuscript, and her impetus to submit portions to literary magazines led to the essay, "Quaking Bogs," being published by *The Healing Muse* in October 2006. As a whole, that first manuscript was tabled, but the essay (now Chapter 31, The Bog) and other segments were revived in *Buoyant.*

One year earlier, in 2005, my cobbled-together kayaking notes led to the Reflection, "Telling Creek Time," published by Sandra Olivetti Martin's *Bay Weekly.* Sandra's willingness to guide me as a new journalist, to not reject outright but suggest edits, gave me the courage and tools to keep writing, leading to over 75 feature stories, reflections, and reviews; four features selected for Best of the Bay. Tom launched my writing; Sandra taught me to refine it.

Nadja Maril, the editor of *What's Up Annapolis/ Eastern Shore*, also believed in me, publishing my feature stories on the Chesapeake's natural history, parks, and farms.

These teachers and editors allowed me early publishing successes which boosted my belief in myself during my transition from teacher to writer.

The following people helped in shaping the present book:

Susan Petrie, the editor of the former Hudson Whitman/Excelsior College Press, showed interest in a previous version of Janet's story in 2016, offering two pages of crucial suggestions. A year later, when I finished a huge rewrite, her press had become defunct, but her guidance lives on in this book.

Lynn Schwartz, my writing coach in 2016, also suggested a style change, writing the story like a novel, but in nonfiction form. This critical move, reinforced by Susan's directions plus fiction workshops at the Bay to Ocean Writer's Conference on Maryland's Eastern Shore, allowed better balance and focus, leading to the book's current version.

Buoyant had direction, purpose, and heart, but I needed readers beyond these teachers. Each has been invaluable.

Minnie Warburton and I met at a Maryland Writers Association meeting in 2009 and developed a critique group. Minnie never minces words but goes straight to what works and what doesn't. She pushed me in needed directions, and when my writing earned her praise, I knew I was on the right track.

Elaine Hoffman's insights kept the story true to itself. Her friendship since our first day at Earlham College in 1975 has made me a better person.

Julie Cadwallader Staub offered clarity and deep spirit, as well as her poet's eye and sensibilities. Her generous critiques have been key to keeping the soul of the book intact.

Patty Holcomb Gavin's impeccable memory helped me recollect our mutual story; her positivity after reading the manuscript encouraged me; her unconditional love, as always, buoyed me.

Sherri Enoksen inspired me to believe in the story's value.

Helen Doherty offered words I needed to hear: "People need this story."

Louise White, Angela Dale, and I have been in a poetry/writing critique group together for six years (Louise originally joining Minnie and me in 2010). When a critique group works, each member elevates the other, both their writing and their self-confidence. Louise lets nothing slide, finds every incongruity and misplaced word. Angela tests each word's merit and detects any impeded flow. Their edits have tightened and strengthened this book; their support and friendship have pulled me out of every writing hole.

This book would not have been possible without the generosity of Janet's family, putting up with my endless questions, and offering memories, photos, and videos that enhanced my understanding of Janet's life. To Steve, Lynn, Donna, and Steph, my heartfelt gratitude and love.

To come full circle, back to Sandra Olivetti Martin, has been a godsend. Her incomparable editing, her advocacy for her writers, and her clarity of vision have made working with her a dream. I am honored to be published by her press, New Bay Books.

Jonathan, my forever love, asked that I simply say: "He kept me well fed." Truth.

The Bog (Ch. 31) was published in a slightly different form, as "Quaking Bogs," in *The Healing Muse* Vol.6, No.1, Fall 2006.

The Author on Her Life

My childhood days were spent roaming the forests and beaches of my southeastern Massachusetts home and weeding our vegetable gardens. Play and chores dominated life for my twin sister Patty and me; our friends a short bike ride away; our grandparents just over a mile past the two-room schoolhouse where we went to first and second grade, past Salvadors Ice Cream (known as The Can because it looked like a giant milk can) where chocolate chip in a sugar cone, Sweet Tarts, and stuffed quahogs were the best. Mom had stopped working as a bank trust clerk when she married and (shock!) had twins, because no woman she knew in the 1950s continued to work after children. Dad designed machines for Continental Screw Company. Both bowled and loved boating, though Dad, without even telling Mom, sold his cabin cruiser three days after we were born. Our two acres held vegetable and flower gardens; apple and peach trees; plus woods, a pond, and a marsh behind to explore to my heart's content.

Transitions led me in directions I never would have imagined. A four-sport varsity jock in high school (we managed to fit in volleyball season after field hockey and basketball and before softball), a bicycle addict, and a physiology/pre-calc/Français-loving student, I followed my Quaker roots and left New England for the first time to venture to Richmond, Indiana and Earlham College.

Four years, three varsity sports (field hockey, basketball, and my new love, lacrosse), a biology degree emphasizing field sciences, and countless friends later, I left Earlham with greater self-confidence and a passion for birding and traveling in the wilderness. I had gone on Southwest Field Studies for my off-campus program, studying natural history, land use management, and experiential education in the grandest of classrooms: the Grand Canyon, Organ Pipe National Monument, Big Bend Texas, and the arboretums, parks and museums in between. This program gave me the skills and nerve to lead Earlham's month-long preterm Water Wilderness canoeing program in Ontario. But it was Dotty Douglas, my senior seminar professor, whose statement after I gave a presentation steered me toward my career: Do you know what a good teacher you are?

Internships banding birds at Manomet Bird Observatory in coastal Massachusetts, teaching at Tatnic Hill School for Environmental Studies in Wells, Maine, and working as an interpretive guide on the North Rim of the Grand Canyon all served me well when I found my calling in high school science teaching at Sandy Spring Friends School in Maryland.

Earlham had given me another gift. Jonathan. After marriage and backpacking the Rockies, Wind River Range, and peaks of Glacier National Park for our honeymoon, we settled back in Maryland where I was teaching, coaching, and leading wilderness trips at Sandy Spring, until graduate school for Jonathan led us to Philadelphia. There, I continued in my same roles at Friends Central.

Two baby daughters enriched our family, and a move to White Salmon, Washington for Jonathan's new job and coaching for me brought new lifelong friends but also the onset of my health problems. I was forced to see myself in other ways besides a jock and wilderness leader. It wasn't easy, and the struggle continued when we moved to Annapolis, Maryland and my renewed teaching career at Sandy Spring was cut short by MS.

Leaving the classroom, kayaking the Chesapeake Bay, and wandering her woodlands and marshes led to another transition I couldn't have predicted: From teacher to writer. To wildlife photographer, world traveler, poet. That girl kicking around the shores of South Dartmouth never would have believed it, but she would have been thrilled.

Dotty Holcomb Doherty
Elated after photographing one of the rarest
eagles in the world, the Madagascar fish eagle.

Photo credit: Jonathan Doherty: Madagascar, 2016

Visit Dotty at: dottyholcombdoherty.com

Adenoid Cystic Carcinoma Research Foundation: accrf.org

The Oral Cancer Foundation: oralcancerfoundation.org

National MS Society: nationalmssociety.org